COMMON WALLS/ PRIVATE HOMES

MULTIRESIDENTIAL DESIGN

COMMON WALLS/ PRIVATE HOMES

MULTIRESIDENTIAL DESIGN

JOHN NOLON
DUO DICKINSON

McGraw-Hill Publishing Company

New York   St. Louis   San Francisco   Auckland   Bogotá
Caracas   Hamburg   Lisbon   London   Madrid   Mexico
Milan   Montreal   New Delhi   Oklahoma City
Paris   San Juan   São Paulo   Singapore
Sydney   Tokyo   Toronto

Library of Congress Cataloging-in-Publication Data

Nolon, John R.
    Common walls/private homes: multiresidential design/John Nolon,
Duo Dickinson.
        p.   cm.
    ISBN 0-07-016819-9
    1. Row houses—United States.   2. Architecture. Modern—20th
century—United States.   I. Dickinson, Duo.   II. Title.
    NA7520.N6 1990
    728′.312′0973—dc20   89-12174
                    CIP

1234567890   HAL/HAL   9543210

ISBN 0-07-016819-9

*The editors for this book were Joel Stein and Dennis Gleason, the
designer was Judith Fletcher Getman in collaboration with Duo
Dickinson, and the production supervisor was Richard A. Ausburn. It
was set in Renaissance by ComCom, Inc.*

Printed and bound by Halliday Lithograph.

*For more information about other McGraw-Hill materials,
call 1-800-2-MCGRAW in the United States. In other
countries, call your nearest McGraw-Hill office.*

"Give us all a reverence for the earth as your own creation, that we may use its resources rightly in the service of others and to your honor and glory."

—The Prayers of the People
(The Book of Common Prayer of the Episcopal Church)

Contents

Foreword

A recent New Yorker cartoon put the situation precisely. It shows the fictional intersection of Madison Avenue and Maple Street. On Madison, leading off to the left, is a familiar image of urbane civility; walls right up to the street, dressed in the carefully studied Renaissance elements (arches, rusticated stone courses, vertically proportioned windows) that were used to create managerial downtowns in the years before the Great Depression. On Maple, leading off to the right just a dozen feet beyond this urbane corner, are single-family houses with gables, shutters, and porches that discretely commandeer clipped, shrubbed, and tree-shaded front lawns; the comforting domestic dream of a New England village with a church tower in the distance.

The point is that these two images, both decades old, need no explanation. They are immediately recognizable as generic components of the American Dream: sets for a political campaign advertisement. The nub of the cartoon is their impossible juxtaposition—and the absence of gridlock, crime, poverty, and disparity. We know what Madison Avenue is like, we know what Maple Street is like; yet we don't know what the actual world is like. We don't know how to depict places that are culturally diverse, that join together living and working, and that bring people together more densely. We don't have commonly understood images of how to build places where people can live close together in a way that is dignified; in a way that can build an inhabitable city.

An inhabitable city is one where life counts. It is a city that is measured in human acts. It is a city that creates an arena for differences, a city that is mysterious. In an inhabitable city, we see ourselves reflected not in stereotypes but in particularities. In an inhabitable city, things are within reach, people are present, minds and emotions are engaged, places are distinct. In such a city festivals make sense. Without proximities these things don't happen.

The examples in this book are proximities. They are the efforts of architects in varying circumstances to come to grips with close-packed living, to meet the challenge of devising the housing types with which our cities will be reformulated. Often this is called "meeting the demands of the market," and, yes, often that is the driving motivation. But this collection shows us that what is expressed in the market is an upheaval in our collective living patterns. The market bears the land costs it does because there is need; because our population is incessantly growing, we are changing how we live, and because the comfortable suburban patterns still being replicated across the countryside are wasteful and disruptive and cannot house the diverse population that we are.

Confronting close-packed organization is a demanding task. There are a host of inventions required. How are individual units identified? What is the sequence for a visitor? How can outlook be controlled to provide privacy yet offer release from the confines of a room? Where can "neighboring" happen in ways that do not intrude on the private realm? How can individual living places receive sun and have a variety of lighting conditions throughout the day? Where do children and adults play? How does a multiple dwelling maintain security? Who sweeps the sidewalks? Perhaps most vexing of all, where do cars go and what then is left of the ground?

On each site, simulated on each architect's drawing board and in each developer's pro forma, these questions create a struggle of priorities. But we must remember that the consequences are greater, that each is a project in the rebuilding of the city.

Grasping the nature of these new forms of housing will allow communities to become proactive. Local jurisdictions need to create the conditions and the restrictions that will bring new forms of housing into their midst. Their challenge is to anticipate ways of building that will construct a coherent but credibly complex public realm, one that provides its citizens with an adequate understanding of the world they live in, as well as a secure sense of their personal worth.

This book provides a valuable foundation for constructing new common sense opportunities, a revision of the city we actually are, in terms that provide the pleasures of lively inhabitation.

DONLYN LYNDON

Introduction

Common Walls/Private Homes characterizes the efforts of some of America's best architects to design private, amenable, and aesthetic forms of attached housing. Twenty-two examples, out of two-hundred examined, have been selected for systematic evaluation. They represent a broad geographical range and serve an even broader group of housing consumers. To our knowledge, this is the first attempt to identify the vast potential of this rapidly evolving architectural form in America.

Innovative forms of attached housing have emerged over the past several years in response to a host of social, demographic, economic, land use, and aesthetic changes. The result is a radical departure from the post-World War II response to sheltering America.

Over the past few years, single-family homes have been engaged in a dramatic race for prominence with attached housing. As small variations in cost and demographic factors occur, the race changes. In the early 1980s, when mortgage interest rates soared, attached housing gained on the single-family leader. Since 1985, with interest rates easing, single-family houses have resumed their historical lead.

One factor fueling demand for the attached form is the scarcity of land in places where development pressures are the greatest. In and around the nation's population centers, prime land for development has largely been used up. In some areas, center-city deterioration has discouraged the development of the little land that is available. As developers look to the suburbs for opportunity, many zoning jurisdictions there have tightened land-use controls, further restricting the supply of buildable land.

The combination of land scarcity and restrictive zoning has placed a premium on land and has inflated values in many areas where demand is high. Unexpectedly, in the 1970s, we seemed no longer to have enough land to realize the American dream of a lot and a home for every middle-class family.

One reaction of the single-family homebuilder is to move further out into the countryside where land is cheaper and zoning less restrictive to provide housing affordable to the middle of the market. The environmental damage and public cost incurred by the resultant construction of roads, bridges, sewer and water systems, shopping centers, and schools have been decried by many.

A better response has been to turn to attached housing, which has become a successful antidote to land scarcity, an environmentally sound and more affordable method of sheltering the nation's population close to jobs, services, and the other amenities of community living.

The new types of homes exemplified by attached housing are also a natural and predictable response to the demand for increased diversity in housing experienced over the past decade. Today, developers must build for singles, childless couples, mobile yuppies, empty nesters, aging rebels, retirees, and the geriatric generation. These groups constitute a host of smaller household types with highly specific needs.

These new home buyers are a dynamic group, looking for a variety of sizes, shapes, styles, and prices of housing. To many of them, the 2500-square-foot ranch in a single-family suburban subdivision runs counter to their needs and taste. Some want a greater sense of community, others fewer maintenance chores or more security. Many want a lower price, a few want more glitter, and some, a shorter distance to the health club or medical center.

Housing is tied as closely to economics as it is to demographics. As mortgage interest rates ebb and flow in response to changes in the national credit markets, the production rate of housing follows in parallel rhythm. As interest rates increase by a single percentage point, hundreds of thousands of potential home buyers become unable to afford an average-priced new home. In years when inflation outpaces increases in real income, the high cost of building materials often prices an even larger segment of the population out of the market.

The market responds, in part, by offering lower-priced houses. The most dramatic method of lowering the costs of houses is to attach them, thus taking advantage of the efficiencies of common walls, shorter sidewalks, fewer linear feet of utility lines, bulk purchase of building materials, and the sharing of land and development costs among a larger number of units. These economic trends have been directly responsible for the increased popularity of attached houses.

Of course, the question that potential buyers, future neighbors, and zoning officials ask is whether attached houses can be designed to fit their expectations and traditions. The more successful examples have answered in the affirmative, building on a long European and more contemporary American experience.

Europe experienced its first surge of massive industrialization in the first seventy years of the nineteenth century. Subsequently, as the labor force migrated from the farm to the city, large numbers of people needed immediate access to a common workplace. The initial urban response was the ghetto, which was dense and built without attention to amenity. Slowly, nineteenth-century European governments recognized the human, social, and economic costs of high-density unplanned projects; eventually regulations were adopted to rectify the most obviously undesirable conditions. Architects of the early twentieth century began to address the issue of high-density housing with a fresh attitude.

The resulting architecture, as evidenced in the Amsterdam housing projects built in the 1910s and 1920s and in the International Exhibition of 1924 in Munich, represents some of the most innovative and sensitive work done in this century. In 1925, Le Corbusier's Plan Voisin fully fleshed out a vision which included the high-density housing now required of a modern metropolis.

America lagged behind Europe in experiencing the crush of population in its urban areas. It has only been in the last forty years that this nation's metropolitan areas have felt the tightening noose of limited land for continued development. American entrepreneurs have responded with row houses, dense tract housing, high-rise apartments, and most recently with cooperatives and condominiums. In the early American response, we see too much unquestioned application of familiar housing forms, creating mute replications, without perspective or innovation. Many of these projects attempt to convey an image of individualized units, but instead form a blanket of undifferentiated building. Such developments present a homogenized vision of human accommodation in direct opposition to the traditional aesthetic values of the American home.

Attempts to accommodate the new density being imposed on metropolitan America have been motivated more by an immediate profit motive than by long-term value and appeal. The gratuitously meandering condo has become the object of public ridicule. Like an awkward adolescent, attached housing in America frequently embarrasses us as an unconsidered response to an immediate need.

Just as the architects of 1924 Amsterdam began to see the possibilities in urban block housing, contemporary American architects are now beginning the process of reevaluating the typical attached-housing project. As American households begin to feel ill-fitted by their present make-do condos or tract houses, the criteria for selecting such a house is changing.

Affordability is paramount, but the long-term economics of energy efficiency, low maintenance, and aesthetic fit is beginning to dominate the concerns of an increasingly educated homeowner's market. Moreover, the level of quality demanded by such homeowners has increased dramatically. The response to these fundamental shifts in vision, for those constructing the next generation of attached-housing projects in the United States, is the donning of a new perspective.

This book, although firmly focused on the responsibility of architects to manage costs and enhance utility, addresses the need for innovation, vision, and high standards in attached housing. To evaluate the examples selected, this book uses a carefully developed set of criteria to answer the logical and immediate questions raised by attached housing. Society wants to know whether this form punctures the American dream; whether it violates the American sense of turf, territoriality, and privacy; and whether it degrades the environment, or, in the alternative, whether it is an enduring response to the diverse needs of a changing society. Each example discussed here is scrutinized using a set of criteria based on such factors as design, land use, provision of amenities, energy efficiency, affordability, and marketability.

The examples are organized into eight categories. They distinguish themselves by the character of their sites, which are challenging or benign or urban in-fill parcels; by the use to which they are put by the elderly, by vacationers, as mixed-use projects, or by lower- or middle-income households; or by the vision they represent, these being projects that have not yet been built, for one reason or another.

This organization provides an opportunity to illustrate the diversity of use of the attached house. These developments, however, not only range across subject matter categories, but across a wide geographical and economic spectrum. In this book, projects are presented from places as distinct as Syracuse and Albuquerque or Boston and San Francisco, and they run the gamut from pristine mountain to urban slum and from startlingly expensive to remarkably affordable.

The attached form of housing, as the examples demonstrate, has proved itself sufficiently potent and flexible to respond positively to the challenge of housing America's changing population in an increasingly vulnerable environment.

An Illustrative Case Study

ARLINGTON COURT

Houston, Texas

William F. Stern and Associates, *Architects*

OBJECTIVES

In evaluating William Stern's Arlington Court development in Houston, Texas, as in evaluating the other projects in this book, a detailed set of criteria was used. These criteria were applied through the use of an extensive questionnaire completed by the architects of each project. The criteria and the questionnaire are included, for the reader's reference, at the end of this book.

As a further attempt to aid the reader in this type of exercise, this discussion of Arlington Court also introduces, and very generally explains, the evaluation standards that serve as the foundation for this book. In analyzing Arlington Court, we inquired, in the broadest possible sense, as to what was the project's overall objective. At root, what was its conceptual basis, its reason for being? Who was it intended to serve, and how was it to meet the needs of those it would serve? Our conclusions follow.

Among the many challenges to contemporary American cities is the need to maintain and attract the middle class. The three decades following the Korean War were not kind to central cities in this respect. Characterized by a presidential commission as the ''thinning out'' of our demography, the middle-class urban population has leap-frogged into suburbia and ex-urbia in unprecedented numbers. A countertrend of irregular occurrence is known as ''gentrification,'' an inapt label for the in-migration of middle-income households to urban neighborhoods.

Where gentrification has occurred, it has been linked generally to youthful adults at the early stages of household formation. Employed in the center city, interested in its pulse and excitement, and anxious for affordability, these new households are willing to accept the challenge of inner-city neighborhood life, with its attendant insecurities.

Figure 1 Site plan. The fully
contiguous alley-side units (ten of the
eighteen total) create enough density to
allow for the division of the street-side
unit into three clusters. The central
promenade-processional axis has a
beginning (gatehouse right), middle
(double shade tree seating areas), and
end (pool).

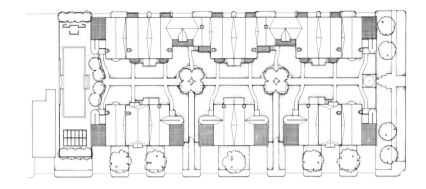

Figure 2 Street facade. Arlington
Court has an aligned array of three
cluster units, ends proudly massed, gaps
used consciously as thresholds to the
courtyard behind.

This trend is threatened by the gradual maturing of the nation's population as the baby boom generation passes through middle age, which favors the further suburbanization of our society. In the 1990s there will be proportionately fewer young-adult households to "gentrify" urban neighborhoods. To the extent that gentrification is desired, American cities will have to increase their pulling power. Central among their assets will be the quality and amenity of the housing stock.

Arlington Court, in Houston, exemplifies a successful attempt to draw the gentrification crowd. In an historic, near-downtown neighborhood, this new development of eighteen dwellings on 1 acre employed several unusual techniques to attract singles, young couples, and some vital empty nesters.

First, it emphasized security and a sense of community. The project was conceived as an enclave, completely protected as a community unto itself. The site was planned so that individual town houses orient toward a pedestrian courtyard, with vehicular access on the perimeter only. The "front door" of the development is a gatehouse, through which a resident or visitor passes while proceeding through the courtyard to the residences.

Second, it featured individual ownership of land, rather than the recent emphasis on rental housing or lesser forms of ownership. The individual units are sold at Arlington Court, along with the underlying land, to the purchaser. This contrasts to condominium ownership, where the land is held in common by the condominium corporation. The theory here is that young adults and empty nesters have grown accustomed to, and prefer, this more complete form of ownership.

Third, and for similar reasons, the units are relatively large for an in-town town house. They range in size from 1600 to 2000 square feet for a two-bedroom unit. This contrasts with the trend, evident in some suburban areas, to downsize town houses for today's smaller-sized households. The units all have two baths which, with the ample size, give them a competitive edge over some outlying houses. This urge to compete is further enhanced by fireplaces, tiled terraces overlooking the street, separate utility rooms, one-third open space, a community lap pool, a covered sitting area, and extended views.

Fourth, price, which is the essence of competition for this market, is kept affordable. This begins with the relatively low cost of land in the near downtown. It is greatly enhanced by the density permitted in the relatively unregulated Houston area. Two parking spaces per unit were required. The building code effectively limited the heights of the buildings. With creative design, a density of eighteen units on the acre to be developed was achieved. This allowed dramatic cost efficiency in the use of the land and infrastructure. Through the repetition of elements (four basic layouts for the eighteen units), the use of standard building products, and the careful monitoring of the budget, costs were further contained. The total cost of construction for this project, which was completed in 1985, was $60 per square foot.

Finally, a true urban community was created at Arlington Court. With garages oriented outward and an interior pedestrian courtyard commanding the site, the sense of density is significantly mitigated. The courtyard plays effectively with individual decks and patios so that the site plan integrates its urban sense with the privacy of the individual unit.

COMMUNITY

Narrowing the focus slightly, we then inquired about the compatibility of Arlington Court with the surrounding neighborhood. How successful were the architect and developer in achieving a conceptual, physical, and aesthetic link between the project and the surrounding space occupied?

3

Figure 3 *Courtyard gate. The extensions and perforations of the end wall create a datum behind which an entry rotunda gatehouse awaits visitors. Note the flanking stair towers and stepped massing beyond heightening the sense of thresholds.*

Figure 4 *Processional entry. Paving pattern, wall, gate, conical roof, and stepping massing relate to the straight-line axis that slices through the entire length of the site. Note the consistent use of a limited palette of materials.*

4

The scale, architecture, and tenure of this development serve to integrate it into the surrounding Houston neighborhood. Arlington Court is located in a neighborhood known as The Heights, which dates from the 1890s and boasts several large historic homes and several streets of bungalows preserved from that era. The development is in the center of the neighborhood and accentuates the architecture of the surrounding area by loosely blending with the style of these older homes without becoming a self-conscious copy. The aesthetics of the project are influenced by such nineteenth-century masters as Richardson and Shaw. Its low-rise massing puts it at or just over the treetops. Some units enjoy long views of downtown. Most have balconies overlooking the street.

The courtyard community created by the architects becomes an urban amenity unto itself. Vehicles approach Arlington Court from Arlington Street on the east and from an alley on the west. Residents and guests walk inside from side gates along Arlington Court and through a gatehouse on the north. The feel is reminiscent of memorable private urban streets, with their gentle buffer from the bustle of the city. One respects the need for this buffer in a residential community that chooses to locate in the heart of an urban area.

The use of the separately owned town house can also be seen as a way of relating to and enhancing the surrounding community. Row housing is a standard presence in near-downtown areas. The town house, of late, has become a favored form of architecture for the new American household. By cloistering these new town houses through careful site planning, a unique adaptation of a familiar motif is achieved. Offering individual ownership of land and building to purchasers tends to reinforce property values in the neighborhood. This ownership form is clearly recognized as the most prestigious form of housing tenure, a fact which would have to be appreciated by nearby property owners.

5

ENVIRONMENT

The essential challenge in the coming decades of preserving and enhancing our environment must be addressed in every attempt to place buildings on land, wherever it is situated. Did the undeveloped site have important environmental features, natural resources worthy of preservation? If so, were they respected, and by what methods? Were natural elements added as part of the development?

The environmental challenges here were minimal. The site had hosted a grocery store and parking lot, without the benefit of any vegetation. There were no notable environmental features, nothing there to preserve or enhance. As distin-

6

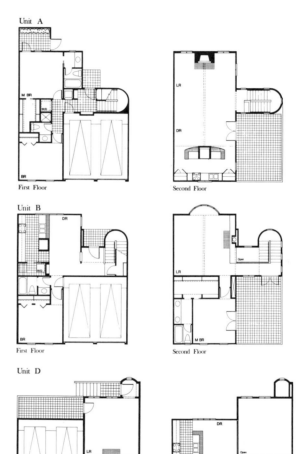

7

Figure 5 *Stair tower. The formal manipulation of the consistent building materials has its ultimate expression of corner in the form of this vertical shape, basking in the sun. Note the levitating gable forms left and sculptural pool gazebo right—all given a placid basis by the pool in the foreground.*

Figure 6 *Axis terminus. Marching buildings give way to the final goal of the site-long axis—the cool blue of the lap pool.*

Figure 7 *Unit plans. Each unit has its own individual atmosphere while using common programmatic elements. Two cars, two bedrooms, and two baths are housed along with ample storage, kitchen, and living space. Each unit has a balcony or terrace and a fireplace. The distinctions between units involve varying the relationships between the dining and living and kitchen areas, as well as the location of bedrooms. Stairs are also crucially distinctive elements, with eight units having semidetached stair towers.*

Photographs Courtesy of the Architect

guished from much suburban development today, there were no wrenching environmental dilemmas such as development on wetlands, on slopes, or in mature woodlands or wildlife habitats. This highlights one of the many advantages of cost-effective in-city development: development where it ought to be.

The site plan creates a strong identity which adds an environmental feature to the neighborhood, a new urban space. The plantings are all indigenous. The axis is north-south, with the courtyard protected from the intense sun by the height of the units. Glass is minimized and cross ventilation is emphasized. The visual orientation is into the courtyard from the living areas.

ORGANIZATION

Looking more specifically at the project that was built, we evaluated its physical organization on the site. In how many ways was the project organized physically, and what is the hierarchical importance of these organizing systems? How are these organizing schemes evidenced?

It is rare that a project of this scale creates a distinct series of exterior spaces, both formal and private. The architect has created an elegant urban bearing wall construction by simply focusing building mass to the back alley side of the site. By creating a three-story block of completely attached units along this street (ten of the eighteen units), the architect allows the Arlington Street side units (the remaining eight) to be subdivided into three clusters. Between these clusters, gates and walls are used to call attention to the gaps and transform these "in-between" spaces into large-scale thresholds to the inner courtyard.

Most site plans in an urban context would leave any further development of such a courtyard to the gardener. But Stern recognizes that in attached housing the architecture can be extended to mesh with the site in ways no single-family house can duplicate. The space defined by the two linear rows of units has its central axis celebrated in three classic recognitions of procession.

First, the entry to the axis is defined by an evocative gatehouse: Created from the same palette of materials as the residential units, the gatehouse is a conically capped cylindrical form sitting behind the exterior flat gateway wall. It serves as a launching pad for the axis the architect has defined between his building forms.

The middle processional aspect of the axis is also heightened in impact by the architect. A simple walk would take care of the need for circulation and backyard definition, but care has been taken to celebrate the sense of path and subsequently defined spaces. The cross axes noted (between the three clusters of units on Arlington) are brought into the courtyard as secondary paths which in turn intersect the central processional walk. A focal tree and surrounding benches provide a gathering place and a pivotal point of spatial distinction. Subdividing the linear expanse into three subareas and terminating the two courtyards between the Arlington blocks, these unpretentious nodes serve a spatial function with a minimum of tools. Secondarily, paths between individual units provide a rigorous rhythm as the axial walk marches toward its destination.

The focal point of the procession ends with a functional bang. Projects of this scale often have site amenities such as a pool, but seldom use them to create large-scale site enrichments. In this project the pool is used to terminate the axis of the central path. A transverse response to the longitudinal thrust of the path, the pool backs up to the end of the site using a tall stucco wall to insulate it and the courtyard from the existing buildings on the rest of the block.

Although budgets and standard materials do not favor curved forms, curves are in evidence in carefully selected places, as threshold conditions (gatehouse, entry wall to pool, stair ends between the detached Arlington units) or as focal points (the subaxial tree, courts, pool walls).

Through this type of innovation in physical organization, with the focus on the act of entry, the process of circulation, and the creation of space in the natural world, this project becomes much more than buildings placed on a site.

INTERIORS, AMENITIES, AND SERVICES

These criteria examine the inner aspect of the development. How are these spaces made livable—in the fullest sense? What impact do these features have on the cost of the project and on the overall physical organization?

Arlington Court aspired to beat the competition for the middle-income market, and so the need for constructed amenities to supplant the benefits of natural splendor was high. The interior organization of the units is varied (four distinct layouts—all mirrored), whimsical (stair towers, balconies, window organization), and high-quality (a bath for each bedroom, fine finishes, fireplaces).

Beyond "laundry lists" of desirable components, care has been taken to create a sense of personalization and ownership. The bedrooms within each unit have separate views, and occasionally are on separate levels. Double-height rooms and cathedral ceilings create a great deal of spatial variety and in fact call attention to the potentials of bearing-wall construction.

8

9

Figure 8 *Living-dining-kitchen. The upper floor of six units is a single cathedral-ceiling defined space combining three disparate functions. The kitchen (right foreground) uses low walls to provide partial distinction. Note the use of local symmetry and the power of the fireplace.*

Figure 9 *Stair tower interior. A marvelously ambiguous space, housing a great deal of air.*

Special attention is paid to the stairs connecting the floors. In half the units, the stairs are expressed as semidetached elements, creating the towerlike forms. The architect uses both the space of the stair and the connection of the stair to the building to create a wholly distinct series of interior spaces.

Besides these overt gestures, the variegated skin of the two rows contains a great variety of spaces particular to each unit plan. Central units (without the end unit's three exterior walls for windows) have a huge, open living-dining-kitchen floor and terrace on the level above the ground plane. Other units separate the dining-kitchen rooms on the ground level with a living room and terrace on the upper level.

All this variety has a central set of design principles. Both light and view are enhanced in three ways. First, all the units raise the bulk of their habitable space above the ground plane using the two-car garages as an integral part of the ground-level floor plan. Secondly, each unit has a balcony or terrace above the din of the street. Lastly, glazing is used judiciously to avoid overheating and yet still provide adequate daylighting to create a sense of open, airy space within the confines of common-wall construction.

This project also makes provisions for security, lawn care, generous storage capacity, and low-maintenance materials.

EFFICIENCY

In this energy-conscious age, evaluation criteria must ask whether any special efforts are made to decrease comsumption and cost while increasing comfort.

Texas is a hot place in the summer. This architect's energy-efficient design provides cross ventilation, proper window placement, and two separate zones for air conditioning to minimize the potential for stressing the heating and cooling systems. Texas is also a place of heavy rains. Metal roofs of good pitch are used to prevent the need for constant maintenance.

DESIGN CONCLUSIONS

This approach to evaluating attached housing helps to understand what Stern and other successful architects do to give these larger buildings an attractive presence and a habitable feeling. A few central principles emerge from Arlington Court that define its considerable success:

1. Exterior space is created.
2. Circulation is thoroughly designed.
3. The natural and contextual surroundings are respected.
4. Distinct thresholds, axes, and focal points are employed.
5. An explicit ordering system is applied.
6. Close attention is paid to material, detail, color, and surface.
7. The needs of the intended occupants are accommodated.
8. Form and facade are integrated.

These principles emerge, time and again, as the succeeding twenty-one attached-housing projects are studied and better understood. They are, in essence, the principles of design that have been uncovered by our study of residential projects which use common walls to create private, hospitable dwellings. These conclusions are discussed, in detail, in Design Conclusions.

Benign Sites

Raw parcels of land, like the two described in this section, that are flat, open, and devoid of difficult site conditions present special challenges to the architect. First, there is no topography to give the development its shape, character, or inspiration. Second, few options are foreclosed. Third, in such an open setting, the temptation is to create too much.

On Wroxton Street and Charleston Place, in Houston and Boca Raton, we see the result of architecture placed on a benign site that results in thoughtful and enriching design. One of these projects presents a design that is essentially new; the other is basically traditional in form.

The architect is thoroughly present in these designs, but the temptation to create a monument to ego on an open site is resisted. The result, in each case, is architecture that embraces the needs of the occupants, enhances the surrounding neighborhood, and creates a clever yet graceful context as an urban place. We learn here that beauty and utility are not dependent on a raging ego or on the heroic defeat of challenging site features.

Aesthetic Variety
Resting on a Brick Plinth

WROXTON STREET TOWNHOUSES

Houston, Texas

William F. Stern and Associates, *Architects*

OBJECTIVES

In an earlier generation, there was a ready way to house a young family: buy a new little home in a development of single-family, detached homes. So it was in suburban Houston. The pre-World War II families of West University Place found just such accommodation in the form of modest masonry cottages built to house those beginning their adult married lives.

But the predictable household demographics of this earlier time have evolved and, today, present developers with an array of mostly smaller household types. With two incomes the norm, children as options, and divorce as commonplace as marriage, a different, more flexible type of home is demanded.

Today's architects and builders have responded to these needs by creating many variations of the common-wall multiple dwelling. This technique was used with remarkable results in the Wroxton Street Townhouses. Rather than build on separate lots, in this land-scarce urban center, the Andover Group development team decided to combine three separate 50 by 100 foot building lots into one developable parcel. It then proposed to double the occupancy to six units, utilizing the fine design skills of architect William F. Stern.

The architect used the community's preference for small cottages and a zoning requirement that 51 percent of exposed building surface be masonry to create common-wall housing with an emphasis on personalized scale and detailing. Although in scale with its cottage neighbors, the units themselves, as expressed internally and externally, achieve a degree of personalization not often found in such medium-density projects. The image of individual homes resting on the brick plinth is perfectly tailored to the relatively wide variety of households the project was intended to attract.

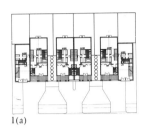
1(a)

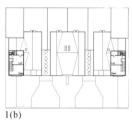
1(b)

Figure 1 *Plans. Garages, kitchens, and living-dining areas lift the building mass above street level (c). Note the entries located between the three double units and the subdivision of the backyards. The middle level (a) reveals the use of street-facing balconies set back from the building's front edge. The top floor (b) consists of the bookend units' lofts.*

Figure 2 *Front. The multimaterial facade, with monolithic plinth and heavily articulated crown, both celebrates its scale and remains a human-scaled project filled with a true feeling of "residential" neighborhood.*

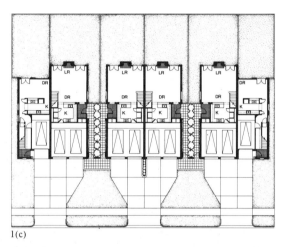
1(c)

2

3

4

Figure 3 *Front/street elevation. The common treatment of the first floor helps distract attention from the ten garage doors while creating a sense of sitewide scale, counterpointed by the multigabled articulations above. Note the variety of materials used and the celebratory entrances.*

Figure 4 *Angled prospect. The brick plinth wraps and the gables are set to and fro, creating a wonderful interplay between the static and the active.*

COMMUNITY

The existing community of about 100,000 people was largely created in the middle third of this century, and was primarily housed in single-family cottages. As this neighborhood grew, it diversified to include town houses and garden apartments to gain a certain measure of density in response to consumer demand.

The architect's design embraces both genres of housing. By unifying three separate common-wall tandem town houses with a continuous first-story brick facade, punctured only by access points for garages and pedestrians, the larger scale of the more recent housing forms was recognized. By animating the top story of living spaces with a variety of roof forms and covered porches, Stern expresses an empathy for the earlier community of single-family cottages.

Such responsive design usually elicits positive regard in the community, which was evidenced in the ease of passing all board hearings and by the sale of a significant percentage of the units before construction began.

ENVIRONMENT

This Texas landscape is flat, minimally forested, and graced with good subsoil conditions. Unwanted solar gain and occasional torrential rains were the two most problematic natural features that the architect encountered. He recognized that the traditional cottage form indigenous to the area responded well to excessive sun and water. When rain falls intensely, the steeply pitched roofscapes and generous gutters and downspouts divert overflow and minimize the threat of flashing failure. The traditional covered porch weds the need for shedding water with shading and resulted here in a delightful architectural combination of form and shadow. By orienting the major glazing to the north and south, the architect avoids the low solar angles of the east and west, further preventing too much solar gain.

The units sit at the street edge, allowing existing pedestrian sidewalks and typical curb cuts to be replicated. The architect minimized the ground cover of the units by placing the three duplexes in close proximity. Private backyards were created for each unit in excess of the 20-foot rear-yard setback requirement.

Similarly, the front-yard setback of the units was increased to allow two cars to use the same curb cut, while keeping the actual garage space completely subsumed within the project's basic building form. By keeping the edge presented to the street crisp, the architect avoided the imposition of the protruding garage or carport form. The prominent accommodation of cars would have violated the existing town house and garden apartment streetscape which surrounds the project.

ORGANIZATION

Essentially, Stern has created three tandem town houses, each sharing a common bearing wall. The brick facade on the ground level is extended across the gaps between the tandem town houses to form double-door gateways. This allows pedestrians to enter the units at the midpoint of the walkway between the double units and creates a dramatically efficient circulation pattern within the four central units. The flanking units are entered off a recess in the brick facade, which also accommodates the garage door.

The first floor is set off as a simple horizontal platform, or datum, using uniformity of material and alignment of the wall plane. This datum is both perforated and eroded by second-story openings. The use of large-scale openings at both levels creates a sense of proportion, detail, and animation not often found in a project of this size. Clapboard siding and the porches and roofscapes above the "wall" create a wonderland of visual and formal activity.

It is the duality of functional masonry and the expressive frosting of light-frame living accommodations that allows a potentially predictable six-unit town-house project to celebrate its form and convey the individuality of its constituent parts. If the project simply presented three identical tandem town houses, then the sense of a greater whole would be compromised. Stern has used large-scale symmetry to counterpoint the horizontal layering already described.

Stern also has expressed the different unit sizes by carefully ordering his large-scale features. Four two-bedroom units are oriented to the center of the project; their front wall is recessed 6 feet from the edge of the brick plinth. The four central units are mirrored versions of two-bedroom town houses. The two flanking units are single-bedroom; their plans also mirror one another, reflecting the symmetry of the project's overall organization. By having their street-side walls pushed out to the plane of the brick plinth, and by having their width narrowed to fit its reduced occupancy load, the face of these end units is inherently different from the expressed porches and recessed walls of the interior units. Stern enhances this difference by adding an additional half level of height at each end and creating a full-unit-wide gable. The result is a framing of the project with two vertical masses, between which four covered porches and two puncturing gateways create a pleasant residential rhythm.

The alignment of the made facade and street and the subsequent formal recessing from the datum presents a third organizing principle. The interaction between the horizontal layering of materials and function when combined with the project's symmetry and parallel orientation to the street greatly expands the sense of scale. These large-scale organizing features allow the project to remain coherent despite the individuality of the tandem sets.

Without such concrete, large-scale design integration, human-scaled elements such as porches and entryways could simply overwhelm the impact of any project

5

6

7

Figure 5 *Kitchen-dining and stair. Simple, open space allows for maximum perception of space. The direct stair helps engender a sense of connection between floors. Note the low wall between kitchen and dining areas, allowing shared light and view, yet maintaining the comfort of functional distinction.*

Figure 6 *Fireplace. Focal point of the living areas, this element is combined with access to, and view of, the backyard beyond this wall. Note the transoms above the doors.*

Figure 7 *End-unit loft. Straightforward stair and balcony are given drama by the loose fit of surrounding walls and diagonal orientation of the windows. Multiple light sources and scaler elements create an active, yet contained, space.*

Photographs Courtesy of the Architect

and dissipate its clarity and image. Without the broad vision on the part of the architect, the act of combining single-family residences into large-scale constructions could be a mindless replication of trivializing components.

INTERIORS, AMENITIES, AND SERVICES

The same care evidenced in the organization of the overall project can be seen in the interior design of these units. The ground floor on the street side is given over to car and pedestrian access. Since urban land is precious, the architect orients the major social and user-intensive spaces to the backyards that are created by the dense unit organization. Through the location of the entire back half of the four central units to living rooms, two walls of each unit gain natural light, circulation is held to the inside wall of the living space, and the living room is allowed to visually embrace the entire backyard. By orienting the circulation and wet core (bath, kitchen) spaces to the middle of the plan, the architect gives the street and backyard spaces full north-south exposure on the second floor.

The single-bedroom units are entered from the street. Stern has joined the stairs of these units with the garages, allowing the backyard orientation to dominate both the dining room on the first floor and the bedroom on the second. The second-floor street-side orientation is given over to the double-height living room. Above that, a loft space offers accommodation for an office or guests.

The two-bedroom unit graphically demonstrates the internal freedom a centrally accessed plan offers, where the perimeter spaces can be entered and served from a double-loaded core. The "bookend" single-bedroom units, on the other hand, are a prime example of end-accessed units where, due to the constrictions of bearing walls, the vertical circulation invades fully half the spaces present. The architect wisely uses the vertical liberation of cathedral ceilings and loft space to decompress the tight plan, while keeping intimate dining and bedroom spaces focused away from the intrusion of the stair. These two basic units provide a diagram for two different interior layouts for any attached-housing project.

This project is concerned with quality and substance in design rather than surface treatments. A simple gypsum wallboard surfacing of all interior parts creates a quiet backdrop for the special focuses discussed earlier. Kitchens and baths have been designed for maximum utility and ease of use. Fireplaces, mostly symbolic in Houston, are employed to signal the living heart of each unit. Covered porches and detailed trim and column work bring the finish level more in line with custom residential work than the average spec-built attached-housing project.

All this took place at a cost in 1984 of $62.50 per square foot. Good design need not be expensive to harbor a sense of custom fit and finish.

EFFICIENCY

In Texas, efficiency is best expressed in terms of keeping the sun from stressing the cooling system. The air temperature of this project is kept in the comfort zone by utilizing an east-west axis to orient glazing away from low, penetrating solar angles. Secondly, the covered porches facing north provide a cool exterior orientation. Thirdly, these units, despite their small size, have two temperature-regulation zones, a useful technique in any climate. Insulation meets federal standards, and the glazing is of high quality.

8

Figure 8 *Entry. The brick plinth/datum breaks down to create a multiply perforated double entry. Note the covered decks above.*

New Forms in a Classic Mold

CHARLESTON PLACE

Boca Raton, Florida

Andres Duany and Elizabeth Plater-Zyberk, *Architects*

OBJECTIVES

One of the crowning ironies of urban America is that many of its most cherished existing neighborhoods could not have been built if contemporary land use standards were applied to them. The combination of density limits and setback, off-street parking, and lot size requirements, if applied today, would legislate away many of our more livable and affordable neighborhoods. Our sensibilities are being numbed by hodgepodge subdivisions and anonymous cluster developments that are the frequent result of the unimaginative application of modern land development standards.

Duany and Plater-Zyberk unabashedly attacked the barriers to the development of traditional neighborhoods in their design of Charleston Place. They were greatly assisted by the cooperation of a benign site and a permitted density of seven units to the acre. With an allowance of 110 houses on 16 acres, they set out to challenge these regulatory standards and to create a classic urban neighborhood.

Because of the architects' creative insight, the regulatory definitions have been transformed. Alleys are substituted for the modern jogging path, streets are widened to create spaces for on-street parking that are labeled parking-areas, the standard central "clubhouse area" is diffused into several accessible park and recreation areas, and the traditional grid development pattern of the neighborhood takes the place of the random patterns that define many modern subdivisions.

In many of today's clustered subdivisions, a bank of town houses, often placed on commonly owned land, replaces a neighborhood of traditional single-family homes. In lieu of that pattern, the architects here have chosen two newer configurations, the zero lot line and the semidetached home, to create the sense of a traditional neighborhood.

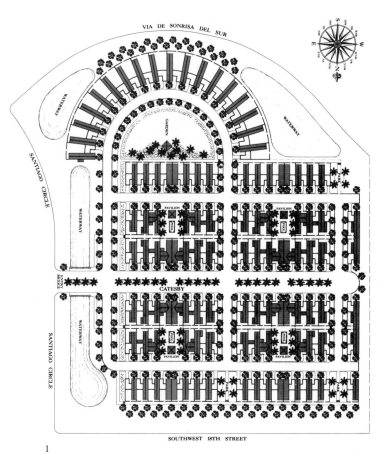

Figure 1 *Site. Four "core blocks" are bound north, south, and west by rows of wall-connected units. A radial array of southerly units helps configure the site plan to the access roads. An easterly minimoat provides a watery transitional layer, spanned by an entry-threshold bridge.*

Figure 2 *Streetscape. Color, volume, and window patterns are varied to enhance a sense of individuality and to reinforce classic residential rhythms.* (Steve Brooke Photograph)

1

2

3

4

5

Figure 3 *Unit. The two-bay structural system has its dimensional variation reinforced by the gable and flat roof form, the functional distinctions of dwelling space and the combination of garage and raised terrace. Rich textures, window organization, and domestic detailing all help lend a sense of scale to the project.*

Figure 4 *Site work. Walls and plantings are carefully choreographed with the architecture and site plan.* (Steve Brook Photograph)

Figure 5 *Porch. Each unit has a shaded area, with paved space and integral garden.* (Steve Brook Photograph)

A "semidetached" home is one which shares a common wall with another home, with the wall sitting on the lot line between them. In this way, both families can enjoy traditional ownership of the lot and the house, while the site benefits from the efficiency of attaching two homes that would otherwise require much more land.

A "zero-lot-line" home is one that has a side wall on one of the lot lines so that an ample yard is created on the other side. When homes are placed on small individual lots with two equal side yards, neither yard is as usable as the larger one created when the house is moved to one of the lot lines. When several houses are moved this way in unison, large accessible spaces are created for each of the owners.

These two lot forms allow the architects to create traditional housing, where a lot and a house are conveyed to the owner. In this way, most of the space in the neighborhood is owned and controlled by individual homeowners, giving legal substance to the architectural goal of creating traditional living patterns.

COMMUNITY AND ENVIRONMENT

The central objective of the architects was to create a classic urban environment, imbued with a sense of community. By using the zero lot line and semidetached ownership pattern, they built several symmetrical blocks around separate organizing principles. The four central blocks frame a broad street with an island full of trees. The project is approached by crossing a bridge, which spans a body of water on the site's perimeter.

All the streets are tree-lined, with sidewalks, brick driveways, yards, and private entrances defining the neighborhood. Most of the street facades are punctuated by a pavilion or small park that provides a gathering place. These neighborhood amenities are supplemented by several others, including the entry bridge, three bodies of water, a large garden, and several areas on the perimeter where trees buffer and help define the neighborhood.

The traditional elements of the neighborhood are most vivid in and around the homes themselves. Most of the homes have outdoor yards or patios, covered garages, private entries, and rooftop terraces. Many back onto a semiprivate alley which provides pedestrian access to a pool and which doubles as the utility corridor.

An environmental feature that is seriously respected by the development is the Florida sun. Its effect is mitigated by stucco exteriors, varied and soft coloration, tree-lined streets, covered shade patios, arbors, bougainvillea-covered alley walkways, and pavilions near accessible pools.

The effect of all this is to capture the integrity, workability, and simplicity of a small-town neighborhood despite the rigidity of applicable codes.

ORGANIZATION

This is the only project in this book where the primary organizing principle is explicitly "tradition," which in this case translates into a creatively applied orthogonal grid. Picking up on the notion that America's traditional small towns, frontiers, and buildings are regulated by rectilinear geometries, the architects have artfully used this notion as the heart and soul of their scheme. "Traditional" in this case is not a synonym for "safe," "boring," or "predictable." Duany and Plater-Zyberk give the concept a fresh face. More than any other project in this book, Charleston Place has utilized what we already have in America: a town aesthetic of extraordinary poignance and utility.

The orthogonal grid is manipulated to form four blocks of equal size creating a cross axis of streets. A secondary layer of units, surrounding three sides of these blocks, is created. The minor street axis extends to form a crescent of units which returns from the central street to connect with the "bottom" edge street on the project's east side.

If this simple street and building mass pattern were left unenhanced, ignorant of its spatial and architectural possibilities, this would be a study in undistinguished architecture. But the architects seized the opportunity to greatly interpret the traditional vision and translate the two-dimensional into formal and spatial reality. In gaining complete control of this project, the architects have displayed a sense of proportion, detail, and movement. The results transform the predictable into the delightful.

First, water is manipulated along with the streetscape and building mass to reinforce the site design. The east edge, the one side of the four-square central block which is unlayered by building, has a minimoat of water stretched across its side, a layer which is bisected by the bridged extension of the major street axis. Water is also applied to each side of the aforementioned crescent of houses.

The second major site-organization focus is space. There are five types of space created by this project, all with functional and scaler reinforcements.

1. *Major Public.*   The inside cup of the crescent forms a public garden—a mini-park—complete with pavilion.

2. *Minor Public.*   Each elongated core block has a central pool and pavilion area, located at the short dimension center. Further, the "top" (west) site corners have small corner parks, and the center of the north, noncrescent layer of units has a similar small park. These three small open spaces serve as threshold conditions and terminate axes, either built or formed by a road. All seven spaces have a natural, traditional locus of center or corner.

3. *Major Processional.*   The traditional organization of a small townscape uses roads as a spatial tool; this concept is clearly defined at Charleston Place with the major cross axes of roads intersecting at the four-square core, while a secondary layer of streets surrounds this core and the crescent swells to use the available land. Virtually all of these "paths" provide pedestrian access. When combined with the small-scale park system and a consistent use of front yards and trees, variety in streetscape is created. The dominant processional axis, the east-west access road, has a double width and planted median: classic small-town devices.

4. *Minor Processional.*   Bisecting the long axis of the crucial blocks and along the back edge of the flanking and crescent rows of houses, alleys have been provided which serve several positive functions: utility access, discretionary access to the pool parks, and a layer of functional separation at the private back side of the units. Arbors and plantings further enhance these areas.

5. *Personal.*   Front yards and backyards are explicitly defined by walls. Gates are used to further define the private sense of space. Above most garage spaces a second-story terrace is created.

Beyond these five basic spatial definitions, Duany and Plater-Zyberk manipulate the massing and orientation of the units to create a rich pattern of shape. When this up-down and in-out massing is combined with a pattern of trees and low walls at the street edge, a rhythmic blending of buildings, nature, and people is created. The architects mirror units at focal points (pool parks and block centers) to create a formal hierarchy in response to all the spatial manipulations described earlier. All front edges of units are aligned, using low walls to connect, while the building mass of the back sides, often addressing the alleys, is staggered, leaving the wall as a detached datum to the path.

In concert with these large-scale spatial and formal considerations, smaller-scale acts of detailing further enrich the architects' design gestures. Color helps distinguish the units. The single-story garage form and the double-height house with its gable face provide a simple duet of form. The system of connecting and

6

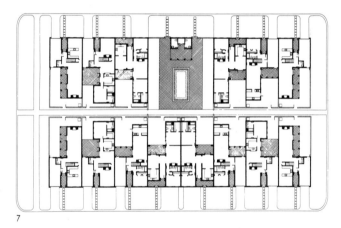

7

8

Figure 6 *Pool. An amenity is afforded each central block. The pool house provides sex-segregated bathrooms.* (Steve Brooks Photograph)

Figure 7 *Block. Fourteen minor variations on a theme create a sense of quiet richness in the unit plans shown in the central block form. Note the central block form, the central walk which harbors all utility access, and the central pool and pool house. All units have enclosed garages and fireplaces. Units around pool are one story, all others are two.*

Figure 8 *Walk. Each central block has this bougainvillea-topped alleyway as a back access and processional celebration.*

Photographs and Drawings Courtesy of the Architect unless Noted

separating walls extends the building's materials and geometries, fusing and distinguishing space and architecture as needed. In fact, almost half the units are linked by these walls only, but the effect is so thoroughly integrated that the sense of attached housing is still in force. Parking is applied to the streets, avoiding open lots which destroy any small town's ambience.

It should be noted that most of these moves are keyed to a benign site. As other projects will show, other site scenarios can preempt many of these artful design intentions. But this project allows full implementation of a design philosophy that embraces integrity over the cheap thrill, and, proportion and detail over arbitrary manipulation. As such, it points the way for a future rooted in our past sensibilities, not as a retarding force, but as a recognition of what makes small-town America so uniquely appealing. This appeal is not to be found in the veneer and pastiche of less successful projects; it is grounded in the familiar, but expressive, structured concepts so artfully evidenced in this development.

INTERIORS, AMENITIES, AND SERVICES

This project is in Florida, and its amenities have much to do with the lifestyle of that region. Water plays a significant role: four pools and pool houses, three lakes, nearby access to the natural salt water. The avoidance of heat can be seen in the use of stucco and covered shade porches, not to mention trees.

But it is in the civic sensibility of Charleston Place that the project distinguishes itself. By utilizing a completely decentralized parking system along the streets, it facilitates a homogeneous sense of community, rather than a sense of density by segregation. By the use of so many site amenities—arbors, parks, gardens, pavilions, gates, walls, trees—a sense of complete design is achieved. Thoughtful landscape design can transform a site's impact from pleasantly benign to deeply delightful. The architectural detailing further brings home the sense of personal accommodation despite the fact that over 100 units and 220 parking spaces are involved.

The units are essentially one- and two-story two-bedroom town houses, each with a covered garage and first-floor public areas. All have fireplaces; most have generous kitchens. Many units have rooftop terraces.

A striking amenity here is that each unit has a legitimate front yard and private rear yard, each of which is separated from the public areas by walls, which in turn integrate them into the building's fabric. These walls serve to enhance security as well as provide aesthetic continuity.

By careful manipulation, significant variety in the design of the units is achieved, and when this internal variety is complemented by the unit and site features discussed above, the primary amenity of this project becomes its small scale. Eschewing the monumental or the trivial, Charleston Place attempts to hold the dignity of the small town paramount.

There is a sense of timeless safe harbor here. Rooted in quiet integrity, a community has been created where the best amenity is the personal sense of fit that most attached-housing projects hold as incidental to a list of appliances and features.

EFFICIENCY

Florida has a warm climate. As such, air conditioning is almost mandatory. But more than air conditioning, this project creates covered shade porches for livable outdoor enjoyment. Bedrooms often have one or two exposed corners, facilitating cross ventilation. And stucco is used throughout: a traditional low-mass heat sink.

Tough Sites

Is the attached-housing form adaptable to the challenge of sites with irregular topography, unusual shapes, and conditions that confound the imagination? Are American architects clever enough to tap the potential of such sites? The next two projects, one in Atlanta, the other in Boston, provide positive answers to these two questions.

In each case, the site presented a tightly constricted context for the architect's work. This happens all too often today as developers consider, then approach, the development of remnant parcels. In an earlier generation, these sites were passed over because other opportunities existed. Today, in many markets, the tough site is the only site. Increasingly, architects are instructed to shoehorn forty units on a half acre, as in Atlanta, or to build in sympathy with highly idiosyncratic surrounding structures, as in Boston.

We learn here, as elsewhere in the book, that attached housing is not rigid and limiting. It can articulate with topography, move with irregular site lines, and respond to the echoes of past architectural statements. Moreover, successful results can seem effortless, so that the passerby simply does not perceive the onerous site that was lurking there when the architect began.

Masters of the Cubic Foot

PIEDMONT ARBORS

Atlanta, Georgia

Taylor & Williams, *Architects*

OBJECTIVES

The size, shape, and location of the site utilized by Taylor & Williams in downtown Atlanta suggested that it be used for unusually small houses to be sold to first-time home buyers. On just over a half acre, the architects elegantly placed forty condominium units ranging in size from a minimal 450 square feet to a modest 850 square feet. Piedmont Arbors is a test of how far architects can go in breaking the residential size barrier to create affordable housing for the urban professional.

Size barriers for residential construction have been articulated and then broken routinely over the past two decades. In the last decade and a half, the size of housing built in this country has been decreasing, with the exception of a few recent years. From the mid-1970s to the mid-1980s, the rate of decrease averaged over 30 square feet per year. In the multifamily, attached-housing industry, architects have worked around minimum sizes ranging from 900 square feet to around 650 square feet, once thought the minimum needed for what American houses have to do.

This subcompact version of the American dream emulated the small, enhanced sports car, appealing to a younger buyer with a different lifestyle. As this trend evolved, several techniques were used to create an exciting product in a smaller, cheaper package. The first, of course, was to create private spaces with common walls by attaching units, one to another. The second was to increase the density at which these well-connected homes were built. And then, inside the units, economies of space were achieved that conformed to the lifestyles of the younger, often professional, occupant.

Architects of this genre became masters of the cubic foot. Interior spaces were reorganized, typically by merging formal dining rooms with kitchens, dens, and

1

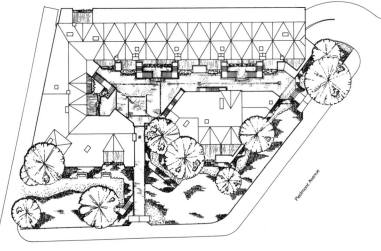

2

Figure 1 *Courtyard prospect. L unit block (left) and "floating" unit block (right), aided by the accommodated tree and weaving picket fence, form a threshold. The distant facade creates local centers and multiple, systematic articulations.*

Figure 2 *Site. Two unit blocks act in concert to create two thresholds and a central courtyard. The skewed site-boundary lines and high-density requirements force the corner units to adapt to the site configuration, creating artful rationalizing justification. Virtually all the L block units are single-story. Only one corner unit, facing Piedmont Avenue, is a ground-accessed duplex.*

living rooms to create a single gathering space, often accented by vaulted ceilings. In the busy lives of young city dwellers, the separate dining room and cloistered kitchen were dispensable, and the open gathering area more suitable to the daily pattern of life. Low-level constructions were frequently used to divide spaces while emphasizing linear sight lines, thereby creating more "apparent" square footage. This effect was furthered by adding skylights, placing windows above eye level, and using light color combinations. Frequently, hallways were eliminated, fewer bathrooms and bedrooms built, appliances downsized, and the washer and dryer stacked.

Piedmont Arbors uses a wide array of such techniques. The small-square-foot units have large spatial volumes, enlarged by grand windows to make them light and airy. High ceilings, lofts, and high windows all add to the feeling of space. Decks and views of an interior courtyard dominated by huge trees are used which enhance the sense of interior volume.

This development achieves the critical objective of affordability through this efficiency of space. The units sold for prices ranging from $42,500 for stacked one-bedroom units to $72,400 for the roomier loft two-bedroom units. Piedmont Arbors was completed in 1984 when inflation and mortgage interest rates had run away for the third time in a decade and a half. During such episodes of high-cost credit, cost-efficient attached housing enjoys special popularity. By the mid-1980s the high cost of credit was compounded by increases in urban land prices which were, in general, nearly twice the rate of inflation.

The premium on affordability was enhanced during this period by the declining rate of savings of most American households which had descended from 9 percent of annual income in the mid-1970s to 5 percent by the date of occupancy of this project. Because of these constraints, the average age of first-time home buyers, nationally, increased from about 25 years of age in 1975 to 32 years at the time of occupancy of Piedmont Arbors. Young, professional individuals and couples, working in downtown Atlanta, were poised by these trends to accept the Piedmont Arbors units with its reasonable prices and volume-oriented design offsetting the remarkably small size.

COMMUNITY

Taylor and Williams respected the Victorian and bungalow styles in the adjacent urban neighborhood, which helped to adjust the 65 unit per acre density to the development's surroundings. This was accomplished through the choice of exterior materials as well as the use of trellises, porches, divided windows, and dormers.

Although the construction uses four stories, the scale is smaller than this height suggests. Since the site pitches away from the street, the first "story," which houses all the needed parking, is largely below grade level. At the fourth level, the constructed volume is scaled down by the architects to a limited percentage of the total available footprint.

The development fits with the downtown in several other ways as well. It puts nighttime and weekend pedestrians on the streets, generally a welcome addition in urban neighborhoods. The existence of urban amenities in the neighborhood took the pressure off of the developer and architect to provide them on site. This effect is reciprocal, since Piedmont Arbors enhances the economics of the city as well. The forty units on 0.6 acre represent a huge relative increase in assessed value for tax purposes. The resulting tax resources are only minimally used by the development. There are no children to be educated, no elderly to be served, and no on-site infrastructure needs not already met by existing municipal systems. The complex interactions of the forty-home community with the neighborhood are nearly all positive.

3(a)

Figure 3 a *and* b, *Gates. Located at the streetscape of an urban project, these outposts of architectural control and focus circulation. They serve as "follies"—architectural "sound bites"—keyed to the fabric employed throughout the project. Gathering the wrapping fence and squeezing the threshold to the site, these two sentinels focus on a local "tower"* (b) *and a gable-face duet* (a). *Note how both avoid trees.*

3(b)

ENVIRONMENT

One of the most positive contributions of the development was that it greatly enhanced a site formerly used as a dump, which harbored twelve valued, but endangered, hardwood trees. By cleaning up and building on the site, the developer relieved the neighborhood of a nuisance. The setback requirements of the city were respected with the happy result of allowing the developer to save all these trees, which the architects used to great advantage.

The principal natural feature of the site, its 12-foot slope from street level, was also turned to the project's advantage. Parking was situated within that recess. By decking over the parking area, the architects created a plaza level, on which the homes were constructed and which gave the project its basic organization.

ORGANIZATION

Piedmont Arbors has four guiding organizational principles, each interdependent.

1. *Site Boundaries.* Situated at a street corner in an urban setting, this project's 0.6-acre lot had major spatial constraints. None of the boundaries was perpendicular to or parallel to any other.

2. *Trees.* Twelve hardwood trees in an urban setting are an extraordinary site amenity. The buildings had to be held off the streetside clusters of trees to ensure their survival.

3. *Bearing-Wall Construction.* The essential unit width was determined by the imposition of parallel common bearing walls through an alignment of the main volume of the unit blocks to a lot line (see criteria 1). All chimney flues, plumbing cores, and internal stairs are integrated with the bearing-wall system.

4. *Density.* Forty units on a 0.6-acre site with preserved trees creates a design imperative that no scheme's organizing principles can ignore.

As discussed earlier, the demographics of the project's occupancy imposed a multistory form on this project, and dictated stacked unit organization. It would be easy for most architects to simply heave a sigh and create a tidy bent block of concise apartments with typical entry cores and repetitive facades. But the monotony and severity of this common approach would prohibit the project from being more than stock fare and would obviate the need to salvage the trees in the first place.

But the trees were saved, and forty units were economically structured and expressively massed within the strict confines described. Implications of these organizing principles are the spice to the design imperative of density imposed on the project.

Essentially this is a two-part scheme combining an L construction and a freestanding building to form a courtyard with two thresholds. All units are set above the recessed parking level, and all the units are predominantly accessed from the courtyard, which forms the roof of the covered parking.

The freestanding building set off the street corner has a multihipped roof covering two "standard" bearing-wall bays and flanking "oddball" end units. These end units utilize beveling walls which parallel one street and accommodate an existing 60-foot maple. The tree-side threshold opens to the courtyard; the streetside threshold opens to a pedestrian walkway between buildings. The L building forms a rectilinear corner to the courtyard. Its long leg parallels a siteline and has nine internal bays of equal width within its length. As with the freestanding building, the ends adjust to the site's irregular geometry. The back side of the short leg rests directly on the site line, causing this leg to widen and creating deeper units with a common-width structural bay. The corner and end units also utilize angular rationalizations to fit the structure to the boundaries.

A secondary layer of construction faces the courtyard and creates the access steps, projected window bays, and on-grade entries. This broken-down layering prevents a three-story building mass from overwhelming the courtyard.

Car access to the below-grade parking is limited to the "blind" corner of the site, away from the best view and courtyard access points. The pedestrian access to this courtyard is quite special. The retained tree buffer to the street is used as an entry threshold for the entire project. Paths become a small-scale forest walk, with their encounter with the street duly recognized with small-scale gateways and picket fences.

Other secondary elements serve to obviate the odd interface between the redundant bearing-wall bay construction and irrational site conditions. Gable-faced roof forms, expressed chimney flues, steps, and bowed bays—all of a common material of cladding, serve to animate the entire assemblage.

This is a project of adaptation. Trees are left untouched, irregular boundaries addressed, residential scale preserved, and a simple structural overlay imposed—all without deleterious effect. Piedmont Arbors is a project where the consistent (exterior surfaces, structure, demographic accommodation) meshes with the inconsistent (site boundaries, trees, courtyard face construction) to create a singularly expressive project. The integrity of the final design is based on the broad view of what was possible rather than what was not.

INTERIORS, AMENITIES, AND SERVICES

These are units for the childless. As such, play space and adult monitoring are not an issue. Similarly, the proximity to a vital urban core preempts much of the need for common amenities.

In this project, much of the aesthetic amenity serves to counteract the density imposed on the site. Most obviously, the trees and courtyard serve to add a naturalist sensibility. Secondarily, the individuality of access to most units—even on the second level—mitigates the sense of common walls and floors. Lastly, a plethora of decks and large-bow bay windows make the outside world both accessible and visually present from within the confines of bearing-wall construction.

Internally, the units are tiny, but innovative in their use of available space. The externalization of interior focus is further enhanced by generous ceilings, 9- to 10-feet tall, and where possible, cathedral ceilings.

Each unit has a fireplace, and eighteen of the forty units have loft spaces, all with their own three-quarters bath. Most units have decks with integral planters. Kitchens are small, mostly galley-style, and closet space is tight.

The exterior detailing of lattice trim, overhangs, divided light glazing, and clapboard facing all serve to enrich the project's exterior presence, which integrates it into the fabric of historic downtown Atlanta.

EFFICIENCY

Any project with so many common walls has a limited surface area and internal air mass. This generic efficiency is enhanced by the use of high-efficiency heat pumps. But this is a southern building, and heat avoidance is indeed the focus of its energy-efficient design. High ceilings mitigate the buildup of heat, and the heavy

4

Figure 4 *Duplex interior. Vertical space, circulation, and architectural elements combine with a cathedral ceiling to create an active sense of home and hearth.*

Photography Copyright 1986
E. Alan McGee/Atlanta

Figure 5 *Courtyard unit interior. Windows are scaled to the spaces they serve, while an inherently intrusive grade-level vantage is mitigated by the screening exterior elements set before the courtyard facades.*

5

gable-eave overhangs help shade the glazing in summer. But the courtyard itself, mostly in shade, catches wind and creates an outdoor room that helps create a civilized natural space that "takes the heat off" interior occupancy in the hot weather. Finally, the existing trees provide a shade to buffer the summer swelter.

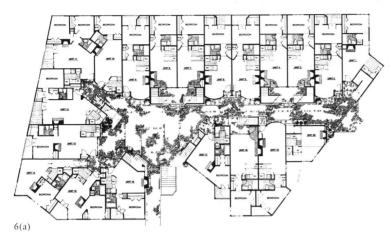

6(a)

Figure 6(a) *Courtyard level. All units are accessed from this level, the bulk of which rests above the parking. Most ground-level units have rear decks. Note the gaps between the "L" unit and the freestanding block (lower right) form thresholds to the central courtyard.*

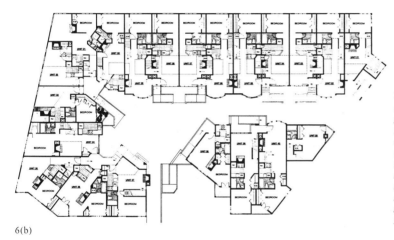

6(b)

Figure 6(b) *Second level. Thirty-nine of the forty units are stacked (with a ground-level single-story unit surmounted by a second-level unit), and all but one of these are duplexes. Nine common stairs, each used by at least two units, project into the courtyard space and act in concert with bay and entry porches to enliven the common exterior space. Note that all units have a fireplace. The dashed lines indicate lofts or bridges above this level.*

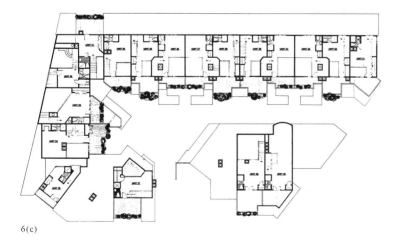

6(c)

Figure 6(c) *Loft level. Eighteen of the units (all but one of the duplexes) has a loft space with a tiny three-quarter bath and small closet. Usable for guests, children, or as offices, these spaces create functional versatility and spatial zest.*

A Resurrection of Nineteenth-Century Architecture to Serve the Needs of the Twenty-First

CHURCH COURT

Boston, Massachusetts

Graham Gund, *Architect*

OBJECTIVES

On this historic, urban in-fill site, Graham Gund created forty-three distinctive living spaces. Surrounded by key landmarks and standing at the Charles River on the approach to Harvard Square, the site had proudly harbored a historic church that had been largely destroyed by fire. Two dramatic facades of the church remained along with a parish row house, which were preserved by the architect and used to inspire the site's redevelopment.

Church Court stands at two major intersections. The first of these is the junction of two of Boston's most prominent streets. Beacon Street is one, which connects several key landmarks including the Old City Hall and Boston Common. Massachusetts Avenue is the other. It passes Symphony Hall and Church Court, crosses the Charles River, runs through MIT and on to Harvard Square. The second intersection is of two important trends in urban planning: the preservation of historic places and the creative utilization of precious pieces of urban turf, sometimes called "in-fill development." The objective of the development, in a phrase, was to enhance each of these crossroads.

The Mount Vernon Church, constructed in 1892 in the Back Bay section of Boston, served an active congregation before it was abandoned in 1971 and then nearly destroyed by fire in 1978. A year later, Graham Gund became the successful bidder on the property, mostly because he had promised to preserve a part of the architectural heritage that the church had offered downtown Boston. Graham Gund Architects, Inc., designed town-house units to fit behind the remaining facades of the old church, planned for the restoration of the original bell tower and the old parish house, and envisioned the construction of a completely new building rising to a height of seven stories from an interior courtyard located behind the historic facades.

1

Figure 1 *Site. Top and left edges of this site and project plan are formed by existing construction. All construction inside these edges is new. The courtyard meshes with the existing tower (upper left) in piazza-campanile fashion. Lower multiunit new construction (right) overlooks the Charles River. Parish hall (lower left) has through-floor units constructed within its shell.*

Figure 2 *Massachusetts Avenue facade. Existing church tower and ebullient new construction "bookend" the classic church gable end.*

2

COMMUNITY

Historically, in the development of Back Bay, corner lots were reserved for civic and religious buildings of special importance. Today, similarly strict architectural and planning controls restrict future development and construction. These controls protect one of the most widely known neighborhoods of nineteenth-century residential architecture in the country. Nearly all the development currently standing in Back Bay was constructed during the period between 1860 and 1900. The images of this late Victorian era architecture are captured and reflected in the preservation and enhancement of the Mount Vernon Church site.

The original rosette windows of both facades have been preserved on the street exposures, and the commanding bell tower has been restored as a single multilevel town house of six floors topped off by an observatory. The original light color of these original buildings has been recaptured by careful cleaning and patching of the original granite and local Roxbury puddingstone. The town houses, which are tucked into the gable-shaped facades of the original church, overlook a garden courtyard.

Through the collaborative work of Graham Gund, Architect, and Carol Johnson & Associates, landscape architects, a marvelous transformation of the space where the main portion of the church once stood has taken place. The architects have opened the graceful arches in the Beacon Street facade to afford passersby a glimpse of a landscaped, interior courtyard. As pedestrians walk along, they soon pass the fully restored parish row house, which rises to the apex of the gable facade of the church. From the other side of Beacon Street, carefully articulated, newly constructed condominiums rise unobtrusively to a level nearly midway between this apex and the top of the original bell tower.

3

Figure 3 *Beacon Street facade. Existing tower and gable (left) and rectory (right) flank new entry. Note that the top of the rectory has two new floors added to its height and that its brick-and-stone color palette is echoed in the new construction.*

Figure 4 *Interface. New brick and revised stone mesh in a duet of distinctive texture. Rich patterning of stone set in the new brick construction helps to create a sympathetic reference to the stone detailing integral with the existing church renovation. The doorway shown is the entry to the gable unit seen at left.*

Figure 5 *After the fire. Before construction, after excavation, this views the bones upon which so much new flesh was hung.* (Photograph Courtesy of the Architect)

Figure 6 *Original. The prefire church. The entire left side addressing the Charles River was destroyed by the fire.* (Photograph Courtesy of the Architect)

4

5

6

This new structure fronts on the Charles River, which runs on the north side of the site, parallel to Beacon Street. Its exterior surface is constructed of granite and several kinds of brick of contemporary design—the total effect being highly reminiscent of the masonry techniques of the Victorian era employed in the restored parish house. From each of the newly constructed units, thirty-four in all, owners have commanding views of the river. Most cars are taken off the street and parked in an underground garage, which is heated, is accessible only with a security card, and is connected to residential floors by elevator.

ENVIRONMENT

The environmental integrity of Church Court stems mainly from its architectural compatibility with its surroundings coupled with its own proud new identity. The development prevented the complete demolition of the facades, bell tower, and parish house. Today, these nearly century-old memoirs stand clean and strong on the streets they have anchored for so long, now framed by the seamless growth of gently textured buildings fronting on the Charles.

For the Charles River, these bold new buildings, which echo the neighborhood's past, continue the extensive Victorian masonry which adorns the riverscape. For Cambridge, this triumph in urban drama stands proudly at the head of Harvard Bridge. For those who treasure city places, Church Court is a monument to successful urban preservation.

ORGANIZATION

This project has a clear triadic organization composed of

1. *The Existing Structures.* The remnant archeology of the church forms two sides of a rectilinear site.
2. *The Views.* New construction has a predominantly view-oriented bias, and forms the other two sides of the site.
3. *The Courtyard.* Created by items 1 and 2, this open space serves to bind and distinguish the constituent parts of the scheme.

Each of the three components has an undeniable appeal, and these appeals are characteristic of many successful housing schemes. The poignant presence of the antique remnant is a testament to the evocative power of the past. The overtly religious countenance of these relic parts gains new meaning when seen in the context of the new development.

The new elements use a bowed broad face, a seven-story ascendance, and numerous protrusions in direct response to the views to the Charles River. By means of the bowing, the interior spaces of the long facade gain a varied prospect from which to address the views. Crescent bay windows and porches create view-focused spaces. The height of the new structure adds appreciably to the large-scale view.

A special aspect of this three-part harmony is the courtyard square that holds the two building components together. This space is the quiet counterpoint to the vibrant built form. The small courtyard is a precious commodity in a sea of urban density, and it adds luster to both old and new project elements.

The architect has detailed his new construction to enhance the unique features of the existing site. When dealing directly with the remaining parts of the church—the tower, the parish house, and the two street-facing gable facades—the

7

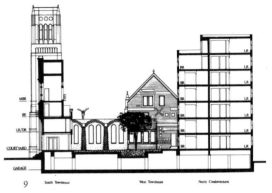

9   South Townhouse   West Townhouse   North Condominium

Figure 7 *Interior. The volume of space and detailing relate directly to the remnant facades which are opposite this space.*

Figure 8 *Windows. A celestial tower living-area displays the combination of old (windows) and new (prefab fireplace); no spec-built new construction could begin to duplicate this type of window treatment.*

Figure 9 *Section. Cut-through gable (left), with new construction set opposite, across the courtyard. Note the through-level parking below all these elements.*

Figure 10 *Top plan. Tower (upper left) stakes out the street corner, while all-new construction forms the two wings addressing it across the courtyard. Note that the lowest unit is newly built upon the existing rectory and that the roof terraces are the roofscapes of projections below this level.*

All photos by Steve Rosenthal unless otherwise noted.

8

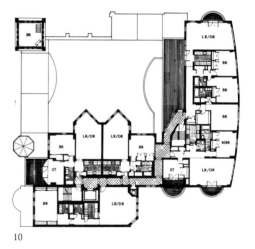

10

architect restores the exteriors to pristine reincarnation and silently weaves new construction within the context of the antique design.

When Gund endeavors to build anew, his forms are derived from the quietest existing component—the parish house. Its brick facade, contrasting stone lintels, trim, and first story offer an approach for the new materials used. Its multistory street-facing bow window seems to be the wellspring of the multitudinous bowed protrusions spawned by this project's new construction. The gap between church and parish hall locates the new central entry used by all the completely new units.

The new buildings celebrate ascendance, and punctuate it with effervescent stone trim, brick patterns, and window rhythms. This expressive verticality is a lyric counterpoint to the somber remnants of the church, whose design in 1891 was intended to be unmistakably ecclesiastic. In a cost-saving gesture, the new apartments are simply stacked plans, with minor variations top and bottom.

The architect tailored the rest of the living units to embrace the remaining church elements. The two gable facades were simply freestanding walls after the fire. Rather than ignore their undeniable presence, Gund integrated the new spaces with the existing window openings. The bell tower was converted into a seven-level folly-for-living. The parish hall was converted to six through-floor apartments: The top two floors were new construction, but their front face was held off to the existing street facade, allowing the existing streetscape to remain undisturbed.

The architect walked the fine line between respect for that which existed and the need to create a new use on a site with a powerful history. Making an exact copy of a Gothic envelope to match the church would set a monastic tone for any housing project. Removing the church remains would be a tragic rejection of a community's history. By bypassing the archeology and creating a fundamentally ignorant building, the project would simply mock its context. Instead of these simplistic answers to the burden of the existing site condition, the architect opted to bind his new building to the fabric of the neighborhood, allowing the new construction's latent aesthetic potential to manifest itself with refreshing zest and energy.

INTERIORS, AMENITIES, AND SERVICES

This project is a model of urban amenity: Twenty-four-hour-a-day security, state-of-the-art appliances, custom kitchens, and fine finishes. The units pay exceptional attention to sound separation. All units are accessible to an elevator. The units woven into the three church remnants have extraordinary spatial variety and use the existing windows imaginatively. The newly constructed units capture the views afforded by this site by means of large windows, roof terraces, and a bowed facade orientation. The project affords a wide variety of unit sizes and plan types. Its versatile programmatic approach matches the diversity of the housing marketplace.

Private parking and central location combine the potential mobility of a suburban lifestyle with the convenience of downtown living. The central court with church-remnant gateway is a unique amenity for a project of any scale.

This celebrated hybrid reincarnation has a unique cachet. Its image holds extraordinary appeal for those who can appreciate its eclectic presence.

EFFICIENCY

This project utilizes the centralized efficiency of a common heat plant with individual thermostats for each unit. Larger units have several zones for maximum efficiency. The air conditioning units are similarly state-of-the-art in terms of the technology employed.

Urban In-fill

In this section we see three architects responding with wit and patience to the difficulties of developing small urban parcels where the architecture has to be fitted into an already tightly woven fabric. All three examples are drawn from San Francisco, which—like all great American cities—is highly diverse. The challenges confronted and surmounted were formidable.

In San Francisco, the undulating flow of the streets, the great diversity of proud neighborhoods, the special needs of its population, and the intense feelings of neighbors about what happens around them are among the considerations that shape the response of the architects. The choices in responding are many.

This profusion of design inputs could easily result in mute replications of the existing building forms. But this would ignore the needs of the occupants and the opportunity to reinvent and transform the context. The projects illustrate how the intended occupancy, specific market-generated features, and the local aesthetic context can create new local landmarks. More important, they show how individuals can be comfortably housed in the urban core and how development can be gracefully accommodated. By accomplishing these dual goals, they and their creators offer great hope for the future of our cities and the conservation of the environment.

A Curving Motif
for a Tiny Urban Site

1083 CLAY STREET

San Francisco, California

Donald MacDonald, *Architects*

OBJECTIVES

Donald MacDonald created a fluid four-story building on Clay Street in San Francisco at an effective density of 104 units an acre. This is urban in-fill at its most dramatic. The site is 4600 square feet large: about one-tenth of an acre. On it, the architect gracefully shoehorned eleven moderately sized units, eleven parking spaces, and a host of amenities. The result is architectural alchemy in an urban in-fill setting.

Both the flowing lines of the city's streets and the scale of the Victorian detailing are mirrored in the building, from its roof line, which mimics the crest of Clay Street, to its window projections, which reinterpret a fundamental element of the surrounding architecture.

One concession to the site's small size, a concession encouraged by the market, is a predominance of small one-bedroom apartments. Beyond that, the building aspires to do it all. Its lower units are oriented toward a rear garden, carved out of the precious ground-level space. Upper-story units face north with views of the Bay, Russian Hill, and Coit Tower. The roof is accessible to unit owners. The unit interiors are as fluid as the building itself. MacDonald perceived the limits that the rectangular lines of the site presented and responded by obliterating them with gracefully flowing curves. This unique geometry, the views, the rear garden, and the rooftop deck all stretch the limits of the site and expand the modest sizes of the units.

Cities themselves also present obstacles to in-fill development. Buffeted by the many consequences of congestion and strident citizen opposition to development, cities often prescribe site development and building-code requirements that are a

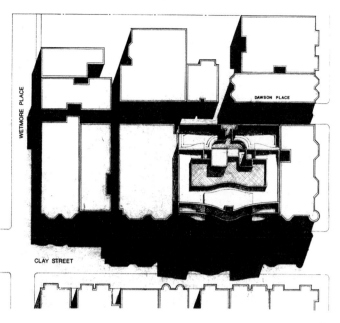

1

2

3

Figure 1 *Site. Set in a slot within the context of a gridded block and back alley (Dawson Place). The side walls of the project adhere to the existing common facade lines, while its projections are restrained by the bay overhangs of surrounding construction. Note the rooftop deck, backyard garden, and recessed top floor indicated by the shading of the built area.*

Figure 2 *Front facade. Existing buildings ascend from three to four stories flanking the site. The new building adds a story to the massing progression, and a fluidly ascendant cornice mimics the sloping site.*

Figure 3 *Front. An interweaving of line, form, material, and space. Clerestory bands slice through waves of facade undulations. Decks recess from the animated facade. Colored stucco top and bottom indicate special conditions and further the facade's animation. Curves are used to reinforce centers, create visual movement, and provide a formal metaphor for the hilly cityscape of San Francisco.*

All Photographs Courtesy of the Architect

formidable challenge to the odd-lot developer. Add to these the multiple mysteries of below-grade excavation, sketchy utility records, and title problems at the acquisition stage, and the enormous challenge of projects like 1083 Clay can be fully appreciated.

One clear application of such limits can be seen at the garage level of the Clay Street development. The feasibility of the entire project was centered on the number of off-street parking spaces that MacDonald was able to provide in this space. The city, trying to alleviate congestion in the streets, required that this developer, like all others, put parking on site. In an in-fill setting, this kind of ruling can be an insurmountable obstacle. There must have been a moment, after countless hours of drafting and engineering, when shouts rang through the architect's office telling all that eleven parking spaces would somehow work and that the project could proceed.

City regulations nearly closed out another aspect of the Clay Street development. MacDonald proposed, and ultimately used, "stick-built" construction, over a concrete garage, making it one of the tallest wood-frame buildings in San Francisco. As it turned out, the city shortly adopted a national model building code which precludes wood construction at this height, making 1083 Clay one of the last of its kind in San Francisco.

COMMUNITY AND ENVIRONMENT

The urban in-fill project challenges the landscape of the city as much as a raw land development does the unfettered terrain of exurbia. In the in-fill context, the environment is the city street and its distinctive ambience. Here, environmental conservation takes on new meaning. Sensitivity to the wishes of the neighbors and to the handiwork of the architects of surrounding buildings takes on all the implications of designing around wetlands and mature forests in the country.

Here again, the architect sets a standard. What more powerful urban context could there be than Nob Hill, three blocks away from Chinatown? The undulating terrain of the city flows up the slope of Clay Street, and the Victorian detailing of the three- and four-story residential structures in the neighborhood radiates all around the site. The architect respects and reinterprets these themes.

Most of the nearby structures have bay windows facing onto the street, with their distinctive design creating a hard line. MacDonald creates a soft new form, but one that fits and was preapproved by neighbors, who were involved in the early design stage.

The heavy appearance of the building's mass is mitigated by the use of step-backs from the ground-floor facade; through the use of the fourth-floor deck, the architect has recessed the middle third of the building. This effect is repeated at the street level, where the recessed entryway becomes a central visual amenity that similarly perforates the structure's mass.

The sweeping and graceful lines of the entryway define the building at the street level. This central feature draws the eye away from the garage doors. The imagination is invited into the building and asked to forget the necessity of vehicular access, just as owners and their guests are invited in by the expressive facade.

ORGANIZATION

No project in this book is more confined by its site; 4600 square feet is little more than the total footage of one suburban house. The site drops a full story in its short dimension. The extraordinary potency of the local environment's aesthetics pre-

4

Figure 4 *Fireplace. Curves in plan and elevation conspire to create a focal point as a grand-scale skylight floats above. Soffits flex, wainscot animates, walls are interrupted, windows punch through trim lines.*

Figure 5 *Interior. Level change, curved wainscot, and dropped soffit all help define spaces that are visually interconnected. The gapped verticals are artful interpretations spawned from the need to hide the back side of upper kitchen cabinets (left). Note the gentle curve of the wall set before the steps (right).*

Figure 6 *Section. Parking and entry at the lowest level, upon which units are stacked. The central entry and kitchen areas are raised. Dropped light-trough soffits further define these spaces. The curved-front bays extend the floor level over the sidewalk while clerestory glazing above the bays is held to the perimeter plane of the building's front face. Note the full-story-level grade shift at the rear of the plan (right) and the even more elevated rear alley beyond.*

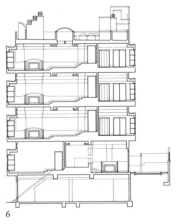

6

5

sents another strong design input. But to put eleven units of housing and parking for as many cars on this postage-stamp-sized lot seems almost foolhardy.

The building the architect created is constructed to fill out the volumetric limits of the planning code, addressing the street edge and projecting extensions over the sidewalk with a similar overhang depth common to the bay windows of the adjacent row houses which flank the site. The rear of the project adheres to the mandatory setback, creating a strip of space addressing the classic back alley, making the mass predictable.

But the most problematic organizing feature of a project of this type and density is circulation. Cars must get on the site, and people must get into the building and then into their units. The first problem was so difficult as to have only one viable (if unconventional) solution. The 60-foot road frontage could allow for only two openings for cars and a legitimate front-door grade access for eleven units. The quiet one-way street allowed for a backing-out parking orientation. So cars are virtually herded through the choke points of street access and nestle tightly in two clusters radiating from the street-access points. Internal structural columns are carefully located to accommodate this oddball, but thoroughly considered, plan. Backing and turning is required, but the end, which is code compliance, is clearly justified by these means. An elevator and laundry are located in the one unoccupied or untraversed portion of the garage. The parking level accommodates the site's slope, allowing the units above to have two walls open to the outside.

Since the elevator and internal bearing lines are greatly affected by the parking accommodation at street level, the upper floors have an automatic point of departure as well. As noted, people must get to their units and, in this case, get up over the car-harboring street level. A central street access point was determined by the flanking garage openings and visually keyed by the use of color. The necessary ascendance up the access stairs lets the entrant off at the back half of the second-floor plan, opposite the elevator, which hugs the back wall. The space between these points becomes the circulation core for the project. A commodious square stair, code-compliant fire escape, and common sink and storage spaces form the vertical datum from which all unit organization occurs.

This back half central core location provided an obvious layout. Two through-floor units flank the core and a wider central unit sits before it. All units gain street-side views, and common circulation space is minimized as the units, not unlike the cars below, belly up to the central access node.

Common bearing walls divide the interior into four bays—each outside bay for the flanking units, two interior bays for the central unit. These planning moves all dictated the embrace of symmetry in facade and unit organization.

These circulatory, volumetric, and planning influences are the core of this ingenious project, but it is the secondary curvilinear appliqué of bay extensions, detailing, and plan elements which is unforgettable. It is as if the constraints of density, access, and site size built up an internal pressure which finds an expressive release in wafting layers of counterflexing lines, walls, and materials. The rigid and the lively interact. All this activity focuses upon the primary facade in any small in-fill project: the street elevation. The banding surface articulation and material interplay are extraordinary.

What might seem distracting artifice gains integrity as this curving motif is brought within the building's volume, embracing plan elements and centered entry conditions. More than any other project in this book, 1083 Clay provides a clear image of the invigorating power of the curve. In so doing, Donald MacDonald has shown the influence of his mentor Herb Greene and has reflected a local precedent—the work of James Francis Dunn in the early 1900s.

The result is a layered building of distinct image. It is responsive to the street's scale, expressive of unit identities, and innovative in its resolution of the mundane problems all in-fill projects must solve.

INTERIORS, AMENITIES, AND SERVICES

The units are not large (around 800 square feet for the 9 one-bedroom units, just over 1300 square feet for the 2 two-bedroom units), but the interiors are lush and evocative. Trim, dropped lighting soffitts, and wainscot are enhanced by the use of color. Elements such as columns, fireplaces, and cabinets are playfully interwoven with an almost art nouveau sensibility.

The two-bedroom units have a separate full bath for each bedroom plus a half bath, allowing for maximum versatility of use. Baths and kitchens are small but well appointed. All units have fireplaces and separate dining areas.

There is a delightful level change running through the units that parallels the street. Essentially the floor-to-floor level is constant, but "back-side" spaces have raised floors, creating cozier bedrooms and opened living spaces with clerestory glazing. Ceilings are held constant, but five total risers, in two groups, allow for three floor levels to distinguish the various spaces created.

Skylight wells are used on the top-floor units, and all units have balconies or access to the backside court. In the middle units, these balconies pull back from the curving facade, creating a large-scale wall animation. The top center unit pulls its entire face back from the facade below, creating a huge balcony accessible from both bedroom and living spaces, accented with a color keyed to the entry at grade level below.

As with most medium-density sloping sites, views are possible, and the top two levels have the added amenity of unrestricted visual access to the sight of surrounding San Francisco.

EFFICIENCY

This inner city does not present formidable environmental challenges, and so compliance to the building code was the primary concern for all insulation and air-treating systems used.

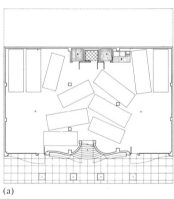
(a)

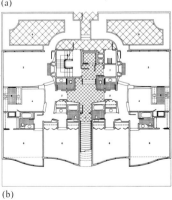
(b)

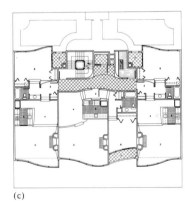
(c)

(d)

Figure 7 *Plans*

(a) *Ground floor. Twin car clusters radiate from the two available garage doors. Back elevator, mechanical, and laundry spaces take up the rest of the available plan. Note that columns (center) are located to accommodate cars.*

(b) *Entry level. Two units flank entry-access stairs. Both address modest patios to the rear. Note how incidental curves help create space while making potentially awkward transitions less problematic.*

(c) *Middle levels. Three units surround the rear service-access core. Entry spaces are up to five risers higher than front spaces. Curves are used to project bays at front, create focal points (fireplaces), and ease transition points in a very tight plan.*

(d) *Top level. The middle front section is recessed to form a wrapping deck while the main and fire stairs (rear) ascend up to a common rooftop terrace. Once again, curves integrate and soften. Note the plethora of skylights (dashed lines).*

Sympathetic Architecture Soothes Neighbors' Troubled Hearts

MACONDRAY LANE

San Francisco, California

Backen, Arrigoni & Ross, Inc., *Architects*

OBJECTIVES

Local governments often shape the design of residential developments. The approval of the local government, in the form of a rezoning, a site plan approval, or a variance, is needed before construction can begin. The impact of a proposed development on the surrounding neighborhood is a legitimate concern of local officials as they exercise their discretion in considering a developer's application for approval. Often, the official view is shaped by the reaction of neighbors. Vehement opposition to a proposal, forcefully expressed, can stop, scale down, or reshape the design of many development proposals.

This is a form of architectural criticism little explored in the literature but painfully familiar to the practicing architect. Whenever a discretionary local approval is needed, the architect must be prepared to explain and defend the various impacts the project will have on the neighborhood. This is particularly the case in populous neighborhoods of architectural distinction. The critics are many and the standards are high.

Such a context faced the developer of Macondray Lane in San Francisco. The first design for the development of luxury rental apartments on this quarter acre in the Russian Hill section of the city was planned to meet all formal city standards, but was effectively opposed by indignant neighbors anyway. They engaged an attorney to articulate their criticism of the initial design, filed suit, and stopped the development. Backen, Arrigoni & Ross were retained, in this litigious atmosphere, to redesign the project.

The architects' primary objective was to win the neighbors' support. To do this they had to develop an understanding and respect for the surrounding architecture

1

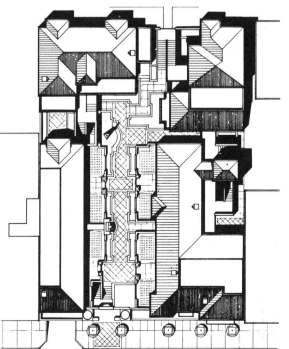

Figure 1 *Project view. The elevated courtyard is a pocket of space filled with rich articulation of surface and forms. The project's gateway (lower left) serves off-street pedestrian traffic and is also the access point for those leaving the underground parking garage, whose entrance is at the lower-left-hand corner of the photo. Note the tall obelisk at the far end of the courtyard opposite the common-entry gateway. Roofs are Mansard forms, lightly sloped.*

Figure 2 *Site. Four buildings laminate the perimeter of a slot of urban space. The slot-within-a-slot courtyard corresponds to the existing alleyway across Union Street, which affords views down to the Bay. Note that circulation in-fills between the units and that the entry threshold to the site axially orients to a triangular obelisk set at the cross-axial point between the long and short axes defined by the spaces between the four distinct buildings.*

and to redesign the development to reflect and enhance it. The result was a stunning success, approved by the neighbors, endorsed by the city, and embraced by the market.

COMMUNITY AND ENVIRONMENT

The design methodology of the Macondry Lane architects was a responsive blend of political, community, and environmental planning combined with architectural massing and detailing. The neighbors were consulted throughout the redesign process. The project was to be built in the north slope section of San Francisco's Russian Hill, a prestigious neighborhood boasting many buildings of architectural merit, several of which have earned landmark status, where views of San Francisco Bay are considered a precious natural resource.

The developer's interest was to provide sixteen luxury apartments to be rented to quality-oriented, urban professional households with one or two persons per family. The apartments were mainly two-bedroom units ranging in size from 1180 to 1600 square feet. The size of the units and market orientation of the development created no problem for the community. The neighbors made it clear that they were interested in appropriate volume, view preservation, architectural variety, compatible details, open-space features, and on-site parking.

In response, the slopes were used to afford views from the site. The zone of vision of up-slope residents was protected by lowering and varying building heights. The buildings were arranged to provide a view corridor at ground level through the site to allow a view toward the bay from the existing buildings on the south. The feel of the street was preserved by developing street facades consistent with those nearby and locating the on-site open space so that it extended an alley way across the street.

This extension became the site's interior courtyard, a major open-space amenity, richly landscaped, with a fountain, terrazzo paving, and detailing that created an inviting neighborhood vest-pocket park, comforting to the eye of the passerby on either of the two streets it connects.

Parking and vehicular access were organized to respond to neighborhood concerns about traffic impact and crowded on-street parking conditions. A single garage was built on the site to accommodate one car per dwelling unit, and no access to key streets was provided to discourage illegal parking and unwanted traffic.

The key component of Macondray Lane is its organization of several buildings into informal groupings which reflect the architectural sensibilities of key buildings of distinction in Russian Hill. The buildings feature slate roofs, stucco walls, sensitive window proportioning, and a terrazzo courtyard which ties the buildings together with a community feeling that echoes the informality and warmth of the site's surroundings.

To accomplish all this, the architects had to obtain a variance from the city's code. When public hearings were held regarding the developer's application for a variance, the neighbors were there in force, this time to endorse the proposal and to lobby for city approval.

ORGANIZATION

Much of the organizational principles evidenced in urban in-fill sites are already woven into the surrounding fabric of the nearby built environment. As already

3

4

Figure 3 *View out. Water views are addressed by the top two floors of the four-story units. Note the private unit entry (lower-left) and private balconies off bedrooms. Existing building at center shows precedent formal manipulations employed by this project.*

Figure 4 *Unit entry. Urns, tile, a round window, and lights all conspire to focus attention and create a sense of individuality.*

mentioned, several strict siting criteria were in place prior to Backen, Arrigoni & Ross coming in to assume to role of architect:

1. The extension of the access alley's space across Union Street to form a court-yard and to reference this site to the existing streetscape.
2. New street facades keyed to those surrounding the site in terms of scale, openings, height, and materials.
3. Preservation of the views from the surrounding buildings and across the site.
4. Need for access to Macondray Lane at the back end of the site.
5. Provision for on-site parking for one car per unit.

Essentially these organizational rules create a contextual straightjacket, going far beyond existing zoning laws. A pandering architect might have kowtowed to pressure and designed the lowest common denominator. But this book focuses on projects that tackled difficult scenarios and came up with extraordinary solutions. In this case, the architects involved recognized the advantages implicit in the long list of site constraints.

First, the imposition of severe height limitations enabled this project to form individually accessed units, which eschew common circulation and entry conditions. Secondly, the insertion of the spatial response to the opposing alleyway facilitated a common public courtyard, which in turn feeds the entries mentioned earlier. Third, the views and the access to Macondray Lane access generated a four-part scheme of unit blocks. As it turned out, each is different in footprint, height, and mass. All these massing moves were presented to the neighborhood in full-scale, on-site mockups, involving prefabricated steel scaffolding. Revisions were made to the preliminary design based upon observations made from the surrounding buildings.

These resonant design impacts have resulted in a personalization of the project's scale. In the rush to maximize density, the chief organizing feature of most urban in-fill projects is the maximum utilization of the available building envelope. The original design for this project had just such an organizing outlook.

Beyond the volumetric requirements, the buildings created in this project utilize an orthogonal bearing-wall system. Most vertical circulation occurs in the three interstitial spaces between the four unit blocks, creating a U of two long units reaching to the street and two corner units at the back side of the lot. The individual unit layouts are defined by their "parent" blocks. The wings of the U harbor elongated two-bedroom units, with central private stairs. The corner units at the back side of the project are clustered in plan organization, with the only three studio apartments located at the one location which does not have the possibility for a view of the San Francisco Bay.

The easterly, downhill block is a simple combination of 2 two-bedroom units sharing a common short wall. This two-story block allows an overview by the upper two stories of the surrounding four-story blocks. All the roofscapes are semi-Mansard in form, involving low-pitch perimeter roofs, with flattened top sides. Upper levels have modest facade articulations: bays, stepping, and projections which effectively preempt the potential for an overwhelming four-story face addressing the interior courtyard. The use of tile on the stucco exteriors creates several small-scale facade developments as well.

Each unit has its own private entry, either by on-grade access via the courtyard, or by elevated access for the upper level of duplexes via interstitial elevators or stairs. It is in the spatial articulation that Macondray Lane shows the potential for inspirational urban development.

Outdoor space is precious in a city. The city resident gives up a sense of personal turf by living within the urban web. By organizing all the units in the

5

Figure 5 *Courtyard. Low-, medium-,
and high-level manipulations of wall
and building forms create a
human-scaled environment. Urns denote
grade-level unit access thresholds. Note
the view of the water through round
gate opening. Note also the obelisk base
at the far right. Facade articulations of
tile, large-scale windows, and bay
projections further diffuse the potential
for a monolithic image.*

Figure 6 *Public interior. Large-scale elements such as stair and fireplace are celebrated by location, material, and detail. Note the modest cathedral ceilings which follow the lines of the low-key Mansard roof.*

Figure 7 *Private interior. Framed bed headboard and cabinet-style closets (left) create a high level of design specificity.*

Figure 8 *Project plan. One level up above the courtyard, the four unit blocks are shown to have different organizing principles. Upper-right-hand corner has three stacked studio apartments. Otherwise all units are two-bedroom duplexes (lower-right and upper-left). The stacked duplexes have private access from the common vertical circulation cores set between or "behind" the units.*

All Photographs Courtesy of the Architect

6

7

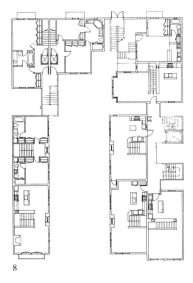

8

project about a central slot of shared space, the architect gave the residents a sense of private ground. A rude alleyway would have simply brought the cityscape right up to each unit's front door.

The courtyard created by Macondray Lane makes a basic site response to a contextual coincidence (the alley opening up across the street) and creates a small wonderland of passage and place. All the precisely scaled elements employed have a common palette of beige stucco and green windows, tile, and ironwork. An inviting gateway focuses access and provides for an elevation of the project's ground level to accommodate the parking level, set below the east side of the site. Each grade-accessed unit has its own walled and gated forecourt. The common thresholds for upper-unit access pinwheel off a slightly widened back end of the processional courtyard. The heavily articulated and rhythmically punctuated courtyard space—involving low walls, ironwork, gardens, planters, gates, tiling, fountain, and a 30-foot copper obelisk—effectively parallels the project's personalization of building mass. Just as the disparate blocks of units adhere to the superimposition of the U organization, these manifold design elements are ordered by the gateway-to-obelisk axis. The wall that is used to allow the east side of the side to be raised above the parking area as the natural contour of the site descends to the east is in truth, a double wall, with a planter between. When its thickness is breached by the focal gateway (flanked by huge brass urn planters), the entire project is given a threshold. In creating a grand-scale focal point in the form of the obelisk, the architect gave all the in-out, up-down surface permutations of the processional courtyard a transcendant organizing feature.

In the design of attached housing the issue of proper proportion can be problematic. Creating personal space can be most difficult in the case of urban projects, which involve buildings that are inherently larger than any scale which might be construed as domestic. By carefully modulating building mass, architects can make people can feel accommodated rather than tolerated by their homes. By acknowledging the larger size of attached-housing projects, which have accompanying large-scale organizing features, the architect can maintain functional and aesthetic clarity amid the manipulation.

INTERIORS, AMENITIES, AND SERVICES

The two-bedroom units are relatively large (up to 1600 square feet) and offer some significant interior amenities. Some bathrooms are extraordinarily equipped. Some have whirlpool baths, others have two separate sink locations. Some showers use glass block enclosures. Other units have two separate full baths, facilitating shared living accommodations by two unrelated people. Kitchens are large; most have islands. Closets are large. Many units have bay extensions. Two units have private elevators.

Surfaces are first-rate. Hardwood floors, cherry kitchen cabinets, copper hoods, Italian light fixtures, and hardwood closets in the European mode all convey a sense of custom accommodation.

No two layouts are alike. The three studio units are small (between 575 and 620 square feet) and are without views. Spatially the top-level units have ceilings that follow the contours of the shallow-pitched roofscape. Most units have dramatically located interior stairs.

Beyond size, finish, and space, most of these units afford the greatest amenity this site has to offer—the dramatic two-way view, north and east, to the Bay. In preserving the community's access to views, this project did not sacrifice its own potential for vistas. Another distinguishing amenity of this particular project is the extraordinary courtyard possessed by all residents. The attention to detail, level of planting, quality of finish, and variety of design elements are outstanding, given that the entire site area is less than one-fourth acre.

The cost per square foot ($148 in 1985) reflects the budgetary impact of such fine attention to detail in the context of downtown construction. But the lessons that this project can teach are not inherently costly. Attention to proportion, detail, and image can maximize the impact per dollar of any project.

EFFICIENCY

Since the project is located on a hillside facing north and east, there is little opportunity for solar heating, but in the benign San Francisco climate this is not a significant liability. The design uses maximum-depth fiberglass batts, individual-unit zoning, and high-efficiency windows to mitigate heating and cooling costs.

Clever Adaptation
for a Special Market

CASTRO COMMON

San Francisco, California

Daniel Solomon and Associates, *Architects*

OBJECTIVES

Castro Common was designed to respond to two uncommon situations: one demographic, the other topographic. Both the site and the intended occupants of the twelve units to be built on it were untraditional.

The site is essentially rectangular, with one corner clipped by the angle of Market Street, adjacent on the north. The rectangle pierces the interior of the block, a deep site, defying traditional site planning. In addition, it slopes nearly a full story away from Market Street. The area surrounding the site is one of San Francisco's many gay-resident neighborhoods. As a result, the market for the houses was highly specific, challenging traditional standards for design and ownership. The architects had to respond to the dual challenges of site and market.

To design for a small niche in the market, Solomon, assisted by Paulett Taggart, had to confront a problem that was presented to architects nationwide: Gay singles and couples differ in several ways from the traditional home-buying household in that, typically, their household size is no larger than two, they seldom have dependents, and they are relatively mobile.

These characteristics are mirrored in the demographic changes of the past two decades. Household size nationally declined from 3.33 persons per household in 1960 to 2.96 in 1980. By 1985, 55 percent of the households in the United States were one- and two-person households. The percentage of householders living alone increased during those two decades from 13.1 to 22.7 percent, and the percentage of total households that were classified "nonfamily households" nearly doubled. Between 1980 and 1985, the total number of unmarried-couple households in the nation increased by about 400,000.

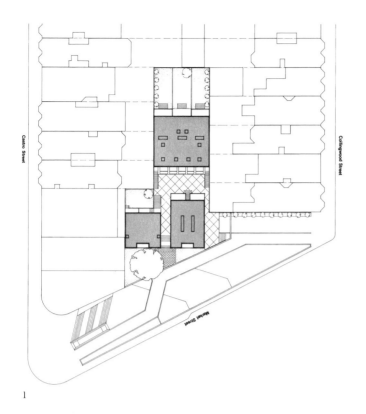

1

Figure 1 *Site. A slot of urban space addresses a diagonal street while interfacing with a sloping site condition. Three buildings are strategically located to create thresholds, define axes, and make space. Note the car access to the lower-right corner of the site and the four private backyards defined by the relationship between building perimeter and lot lines.*

Figure 2 *Project axonometric. The three buildings, linked by architectural elements and axial relationships, fill a void in the urban fabric, while the detached screen-wall rationalizes the front edge.*

Figure 3 *Entry. Building form and street-edge find linkage at the axial connection of the two front buildings. Note top-level cornice connection between buildings.*

2

3

Developers across the nation are confronted by the challenge of configuring their product to the new shelter preferences caused by this change in population. Married couples without children, empty nesters, widows and widowers, gay couples, individuals, single-parent households, elderly parents living with an unmarried middle-aged child, divorced people living alone and together—all these describe an explosion in lifestyle alternatives and specialized needs which challenge architects.

Solomon and Taggart responded by offering the market 6 one-bedroom and 6 two-bedroom units averaging just over 1000 square feet. The two-bedroom models are "tandem town houses" containing equal master bedrooms and baths, configured around shared common space for living, cooking, and dining. This approach can be used for a variety of two-person households where both individuals desire privacy and yet can compatibly share common space. It presents them with an alternative method of addressing affordability and obtaining financing. A variety of coownership and rental arrangements can be put together that allow two breadwinners to combine financial resources to afford today's new home prices. Builders have designed single-family homes using this tandem bedroom-and-bath approach, to appeal to similar market niches in less urban marketplaces.

The architects' response to the difficulties presented by the site were similarly unique. The problem here was a historical one, unique to San Francisco. John Jacque Vioget surveyed San Francisco in 1837. Being a Swiss engineer, he was assuredly precise. As a resident of Chile, he brought with him Spanish methods of civic planning: the use of a base unit of measurement called a "vara," creating an orthogonal grid with a 2-foot 9-inch dimension. Unfortunately, a cartesian grid does not accurately describe the natural world, particularly in hilly San Francisco, no matter how precise and consistent the method of description.

What resulted from this misfit between measure and what was measured are some strange building sites. The site for Castro Common is just such an oddball lot. Facing a major thoroughfare (Market Street) and flanked by commercial and residential buildings, the site is a slot; reaching back into the block, the building terminates the backyards of the flanking lots. All these surrounding properties are of the fixed 100 by 150 vara size, with the Market Street end of the lot paralleling the skewed line of the major road. The resulting site has a relatively small and skewed road frontage, presenting unique pedestrian and vehicular access problems.

The architects' response was to create tandem buildings in three layers, organized around three outdoor common spaces. Horizontally and vertically the design allows smooth visual and pedestrian communication, with privacy increasing toward the rear of the lot and as the individual units are approached. The skewed building line along Market Street is respected by a visually permeable security trellis. The front and middle courtyards are visible from the street. The result is a development that is open to the dynamics of the surrounding neighborhood while conveying respect for its occupants' need for privacy.

COMMUNITY AND ENVIRONMENT

Clearly, a third objective of the architects here was to blend the development in with the neighborhood, defined by a dynamic gay commercial district on the east and a more traditional older residential neighborhood of white clapboard homes on the west. Using a technique that is employed increasingly to win neighborhood support, they sought design approval from an active neighborhood organization.

The responsiveness of the project begins with its name, which is drawn from the Castro neighborhood. The development represents a modern revival of the traditional San Francisco courtyard motif, recently forgotten in a time of intense and extensive development. The pattern of creating neighborhoods of row houses featuring alleys and interior courts is continued by this project. Detailing from the nearby neighborhood is picked up, such as white clapboarding, trellis paneling, decks, and railings.

The skewed street line along Market is held by the trellis paneling, while perpendicular access for vehicles to Collingwood Street is allowed by the site plan. The visual permeability of the site enhances the view from the street and adds interest for the passerby. The lone big tree on the site was preserved, emphasizing the architects' interest in preserving the urban environment into which this unique building was so artfully inserted.

ORGANIZATION

Solomon has avoided a slavish response to the site's primary edge, Market Street, by respecting the orthogonal street grid, which created three rectilinear forms organized to accomplish three tasks.

First, the juxtaposition of these blocks creates distinct entry conditions. The front two blocks (which sit above the on-site parking) house triplex units, and although one block's depth is limited by the site lines, the units present two identical facades, with street entries to the units centered on each. A celebratory entry is created between these units. It provides access to the rear courtyard, which is set between the front units and the back block. Lastly, a side entry to the same courtyard is created to the north of a neighbor's backyard wall to create a simple threshold condition.

As it creates thresholds, this project also creates spaces to respond to the circulation sequence imposed on the site. Several types of spaces are created by the careful orientation of the three built forms in coincidence with the dominant grid and skewed street. Forecourt space is determined by the angled edge of Market Street: Solomon uses a large masonry datum wall (simply a 1½-story frame of square openings defining a large-scale lattice) to parallel the street's line. The lattice provides a secure gateway and carries on the scale of the adjacent bank facade. Set behind this transparent edge is the 3½-story face of the two front-unit clusters. By connecting their forms at the top story (forming another square opening between the units), the architects have linked the datum and two forms at the major threshold to the rear court discussed earlier.

It is the enclosed space, the reinterpretation of the classic San Francisco urban courtyard, that is the heart of this project. Here, density does not preclude delight. By nature, multiunit housing inherently involves crowding. But a good design can focus attention on the available outdoor space, enhancing and redefining it, to the point where the perception of density disappears. What remains is a sunny outdoor "room" addressed by large windows and terraces. These terraces, used for private areas and unit access, help the occupants share the courtyard space while precluding loss of privacy through the creation of an elevated buffer. The last space created is another San Francisco classic, the walled rear garden—this one set behind the back unit, serving three ground-level duplexes.

Structurally the project is ordered by a cogent system of parallel bearing walls—the architect tacks on steps, balconies, and minor formal manipulations to these walls. He then adds a series of connecting pieces, recesses, and double-height openings—all rectilinear—to animate and personalize the entire ambience of the project.

The solitary tree is preserved, set between the screen datum and the front facade. Most facade openings are controlled by the vertical module of the clapboard siding—a material chosen for its local precedence.

4

Figure 4 *Streetscape. Aligned grid-wall extends the corner bank plane, allowing a looming, detached construction to be distinct from its context. Note the expressively trapped tree, held between the wall and the building. The far right building is not part of the project.*

Figure 5 *Datum/form. A grid-wall and rational form bypass each other, with only axial coincidence and geometric sympathy connecting them.*

Figure 6 *Courtyard. As seen from the vantage of a raised terrace, a variegated facade of projections, recesses, steps, and window patterns add life and personality to a focal space.*

5

6

This project respects a macro grid and micro materials, but its form and organization are completely contemporary. Its modernist sensibilities create a focused, centered common entry, a lush courtyard, and isolated garden space. Innovation is not inherently rejectionist. The scale, space, and material of preceding architecture can be integrated into a building type which is unprecedented in local housing forms.

In accepting the 150-year-old design elements of grid, courtyard, and material, the architect has locked this project into the site, freeing up the subsequent manipulations of form and glazing. A thoroughly "new" complex results, but one that carries on the best traditions of its context. Difference for difference's sake creates dissonance. Difference rooted in precedent can enrich any design.

INTERIORS, AMENITIES, AND SERVICES

The alternative lifestyles this project embraces key the list of amenities. Gay people who live together rarely have children in the household, and the high level of autonomy of the individuals involved often creates the need for two master bedroom suites within a two-bedroom unit. Castro Commons responded with slightly larger than normal proportion of bedroom and bath space in comparison to the common areas.

Two site design features also impact on the nature of the project's interiors and amenities. First, the tight width of the site progresses back from Market Street making it difficult to get natural light to penetrate the units. Since all use common bearing walls, and most units address the common courtyard, light had to compete with both structure and privacy. Skylights, light wells, clerestory windows, double-height spaces, and balconies were used to catch light from above or from the courtyard without compromising the unit's interior sensibilities. Additionally, the connection to the units from the outside world is made into a series of expressive sequences. Centered threshold of lattice opening, axial walk, expressive stair, and covered entries are all used to give each unit its own entry *marche.* Although units are redundant within each of the three blocks, these interior and entry features combine to give each of the twelve units individuality. This amenity is achieved

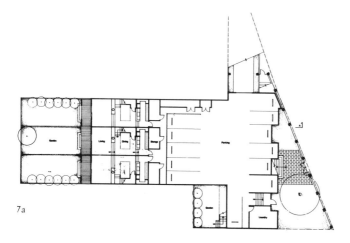

7a

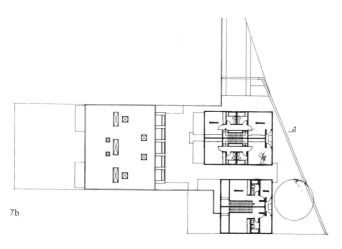

7b

Figure 7 *Plans*

(a) *Lower level. All parking is set below the courtyard and front-two unit blocks. Lower-level back units are directly accessed from the garage, while other units offer access from the common stair located at the lower right. Car access is from the upper right.*

(b) *Upper level. Typical unit bedroom areas are shown in this plan, each bedroom having its own full bath. Note the shared terraces addressing the street.*

Figure 8 *Interior. This particular space centers its window on the entry axis, as seen from the top-floor back-unit block. Unit entry is seen at left. Skylight and window array create a space-defining duet.*

Photographs Courtesy of the Architect

8

without gratuitous massing permutations which would have precluded the positive spaces the architect created between the unit blocks.

Secondly, Solomon has used the slope of the site to create further amenity. Covered, secure parking is a plus which is hard to justify in terms of cost, unless the slope of the site precludes costly access problems. Here the site affords a high corner, with easy access to the street. The building is easily (and almost invisibly) raised to accommodate twelve spaces below the two front-unit blocks—with the access drive out of sight, recessed, and off to the north. Grade is again employed where the common axial entry to the courtyard is raised at its threshold to get above the parking level just described, elevating and separating the entire courtyard from street level. The very busy street is further separated from the courtyard by the use of the lattice screen mentioned earlier. The back-unit block interiors respond to site grade conditions as well, stepping down, internally, to the grade.

It can be said that in the best of all worlds, large-scale organizing features can be used as project amenities; this is the case for Castro Commons. The datum-screen provides security; the forecourt (with tree), the interior courtyard, and the gardens are a gift to the residents; and the use of the dominant grid creates the sort of exposures and entry sequences no arbitrary localized system of organization can match. When these large-scale amenities are combined with increased bedroom and bath space, well-designed kitchens, ever-present balconies, and the fine glazing systems already mentioned, this is an uncompromised project of significant appeal.

EFFICIENCY

San Francisco is not a climate of extremes. Therefore there is little impetus to use energy-conserving systems or extraordinary insulation. In fact, low-efficiency electric baseboard heat is employed, and glazing, by necessity, is placed predominantly east and west, disregarding possible gain or loss.

There is one minor energy payback inherent in an amenity already discussed. With the use of light wells for lower units, clerestory, and skylight glazing, the need for artificial lighting is greatly reduced.

Mixed Use

Historically in this country, villages have blended shops, services, and residences. There have been times when the most prestigious residential address was downtown, near cultural attractions, convenience, and service. The blend of uses, and the efficient balance it creates, has been discouraged in much of America by the rigid separation of use that zoning laws foster. New technology and innovative architecture are emerging that challenges this thinking and provides powerful new ideas about how people can be placed in greater proximity to their jobs, libraries, and retailers.

In the single example presented in this section, homes, offices, and shops peacefully coexist in a small-town atmosphere. Here the commute is a flight of stairs, outdoor spaces are activated by visitors, and shops have reason to stay open in the evenings. The economic and environmental integration of mixed-use development, in the hands of creative architects and savvy developers, is an old idea whose time has come again.

A Blend of Uses
to Balance a Neighborhood

TWO WORLDS

Mountain View, California

Donald MacDonald, *Architect*

OBJECTIVES

In 1926, the U.S. Supreme Court upheld the constitutionality of local zoning. In the case of *Euclid v. Ambler Realty Co.* the court approved a small Ohio city's ordinance, which strictly separated residential, commercial, and industrial uses from one another. Over time, "Euclidian zoning" spread throughout the United States, encouraging communities to adopt rather inflexible zoning districts which separated distinct uses and framed our thinking about American city planning.

In recent times, more flexible zoning techniques have evolved in response to creative site planning, advanced technology, and changing needs. The concept of developers Walter Harrington and Alexander Kulakoff and of architect Donald MacDonald for this 4-acre site in Mountain View, California, challenged the zoning code's separation of the site into two distinct uses, one commercial, the other residential. They proposed rezoning the site as a mixed-use district, which would allow them to build an integrated commercial and residential community in the middle of a suburban neighborhood. The motif is intentionally that of a European village.

The site is located a long mile from the suburban downtown and 2 miles from a major regional shopping center. The 4-acre parcel encompassed an entire city block, allowing MacDonald ample room to plan for local needs. The need for balanced development was as apparent in Mountain View as it is in most suburbs. With this need in mind, the developers decided to tuck commercial development into the site and, thereby, into the neighborhood. This would have the effect of rationalizing traffic, shopping, and residential patterns. The commercial space was occupied by both retail and professional users, with about a quarter of the space being sold to residents, reducing their commute to an short walk. The economies,

1

Figure 1 *Site plans*

The units at the top of the plan are residential, those at the bottom are commercial, with a through-site access road. The unit cluster orientations were designed to avoid mature trees. There are several public and private courtyards between clusters, with planters and pathways creating threshold conditions. The multitude of columns support residentially oriented terraces above, while creating subspaces for the commercial units.

Figure 2 *Bird's eye. Clusters meander about trees, creating courtyards, terraces, parking, and access roads.*

Figure 3 *Commercial level. Ground-level commercial spaces address the courtyard with meandering paths connecting them to parking and the street. Private terraces are separated from this activated level via trellis extensions, planters, and their cantilevered ascendance. Note the heavy structural articulation of the terrace supports and the framed semi-Victorian detailing of these commercial facades.*

2

3

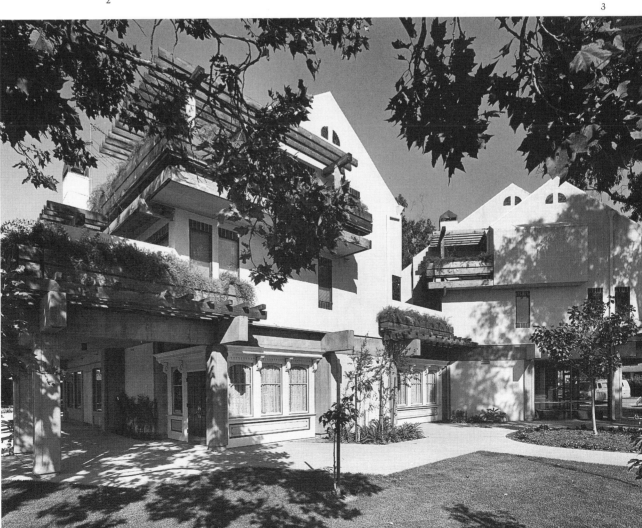

community benefits, and environmental efficiencies inherent in the integration of these uses are self-evident.

The concept proved its political acceptability by gaining the requested mixed-use rezoning. More dramatically, it won acceptance in the marketplace by selling out in record time. The sixty-two townhouse units, 81,000 square feet of residential space, were sold as condominiums as quickly as they were put on the market. Twenty percent of the building on the site, 20,000 square feet of commercial space, was divided into small, individual spaces with widths the same as the town houses. These units were also sold as condominiums. This mixed-use condominium development involved a relatively new legal notion of ownership which brought an additional element of unity to the development. All the commercial units were sold within a year of completion. This success has encouraged the developer to build several more projects, patterned after the Two Worlds prototype.

Through integrated planning and unity of ownership, the developer and architect created one neighborhood, proving that two, or more, worlds can be combined and accepted by the neighbors and the market.

COMMUNITY

The acceptance of Two Worlds by the neighborhood was furthered by several clever site-planning techniques. First, the commercial spaces were oriented toward El Camino Real, a major thoroughfare adjacent to the site. Most of the residences were built on top of the commercial buildings, oriented to the El Camino Real frontage. The vehicular access points for both commercial and residential purposes were placed on, or near to, this thoroughfare so as not to impact or disrupt the nearby residential neighborhood. MacDonald placed wood-framed town houses on grade toward the rear of the site, adjacent to older, single-family homes across the street. In this way, density, intensity of use, and volume descended from the active front of the 4-acre site to its passive rear.

Many of the town houses were built on top of a concrete plaza covering the commercial condominiums. This concrete plaza serves the historical purpose of the zoning district line, separating disparate uses. The concrete creates a firm physical separation as well as a visual and sound barrier. MacDonald organized the residential town houses on the concrete plaza to render their effect on the neighborhood as gentle as possible. They were placed in discrete islands separated from one another so that their bulk was carefully managed. The islands themselves are buffered with trellising, benches, planters, and landscaping, accomplishing the dual objectives of providing privacy for the residents and screening of the construction from the neighborhood.

ENVIRONMENT

Two Worlds provides a valuable lesson in environmental conservation. The slow spreading out of development across the suburban landscape in disorganized or monotonous patterns creates great environmental damage, not the least of which is the long commute which consumes petroleum, fouls the air, and disorganizes traditional community living patterns. The architect's design is an antidote to such ills. These models use existing space and infrastructure efficiently and create exciting places to live and work which, in turn, could reverse the trend toward suburban sprawl and the leap-frog development into exurbia.

In smaller ways, the environment is respected in the project's implementation. All of the forty or so mature trees on the vacant site—including redwood, oak, and eucalyptus—were retained. A full 50 percent of the site is left natural or in open plazas, greatly mitigating the effect of over 100,000 square feet of building and 204 parking spaces. Landscaping, natural wood trellises, and irrigated planters heighten this effect and give the development an organic feeling when viewed from the perimeter.

ORGANIZATION

The Two World's site is a 4-acre city block, bounded by streets. Its perimeter is roughly square. Within this placid context, the buildings seem to be cast about haphazardly. But, the perceived chaos has more to do with the viewer's distraction than with a project's organization. As with all successful designs, large and small, the solid underpinnings of order can correct any chaotic impression this project's initial image might convey.

MacDonald has meticulously preserved the forty existing "heritage" trees which form the ordering system all structures respect. It's always easier and cheaper to remove all vegetation from a site and start anew. But in the perception of a good architect, trees are absolutely crucial in ways both large and small. Like a family heirloom, an ancient tree has an appeal that is at once tangible and mystic. Its tangible gifts of shade, shelter, and soil stabilization are enhanced by the inspiration of its ascendant, organic form and by the sense that it harbors history we simply cannot know.

The square city block provides a hard-edged perimeter for the weaving masses of units to play against. A series of thresholds and raised courtyards work with three grade-level parking lots to organize the spaces between the scattered buildings. The result is a sense of "positive" space, rather than the leftover space found in truly random site plans.

The sectional organization of ground-level commercial and car space dominates most of the project's site. The relegation of living units to the upper areas adds another layer of activity to help organize the site. An unevenly applied, but redundant, hexagonal grid is also used to organize paving patterns and courtyard spaces. Finally, the consistent nature of the buildings' materials and geometries helps organize the scattered forms of the architect's site plan.

This particular project lends itself to a unique organizational model: functional integration. Its name, "Two Worlds," implies a unique conception: interdependent functions of living and working, sharing infrastructure, segregating residents from visitors.

INTERIORS, AMENITIES, AND SERVICES

The nature of Two Worlds' occupied spaces is greatly affected by its integrated, dual-function organization. Two-bedroom units sit above commercial properties, while three-bedroom units sit on the ground. All units are duplexes. Six different unit types comprise the sixty-two total residential units. Twenty units have three bedrooms and two and a half baths. At 1480 square feet, they are models of efficient space planning. The two-bedroom two-bath units are even more efficient, ranging from 1194 to 1288 square feet.

These economies of space are effected by simple means. Circulation between plan components is limited to a tiny percentage of the floor plan. If the crunch to make the units fit the available footprint resulted in a pinched, congested series of spaces, the project would not have received the extraordinary success in the marketplace recounted earlier.

The fruit of thoughtful space planning can best be seen in the project's building sections, where large decks, massive trellises, and large-scale glazing extend the perceived perimeter of each unit well beyond its limited footprint. Skylights work to provide internal spatial release as well.

Most units have fireplaces. Bathrooms and kitchens are simple, scaled to moderate-sized families. Oak floors, cathedral ceilings, and usable attic space all add to the sense of finish and utility. Colors are used to reflect light into courtyards, to add visual "spice" to the roofscape, and to create organic, wooden counterpoints to the stucco skin of the building.

The most important amenities in this project are present in the meandering pedestrian-level walkways and courtyards. Circulation is literally celebrated in this bilevel project, turning a simple path into a series of thresholds, defined exterior "rooms," and focal points. Every "airborn" unit over commercial space has its own "yard" in the form of a deck with plantings.

The multitude of surface treatments, both on the buildings' exterior and in the paving, creates a sense of depth and intrigue in a potentially predictable design. Cantilevered "saddlebag" atriums, trellises, and decks further enliven the exteriors. Lush plantings set in integral deck planters further soften the ragged organization of built components.

4

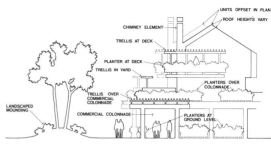

TYPICAL END ELEVATION OF UNIT NEAR GREGORY LANE
SHOWING CASCADING SILHOUETTE

6

Figure 4 *Unit block. Seen from a second-floor vantage, this typical block uses a consistent palette of materials, details, and geometries. Elements (such as windows, chimney, terraces) are subtly varied to activate the block and particularize the units.*

Figure 5 *Section. Layers of applied parts, landscaping, and activity mesh to create a highly activated collection of elements and functions.*

Figure 6 *Trellis-terrace. A secondary system of aggrandized first-floor structural support, and multiple subsystems of support, shading devices, opaque walls, and planters. Serving as an aesthetic counterpoint to the stucco unit form, this natural wood layering effectively insulates the worlds of home and business from each other, yet allows full exposure of all levels to the outside world.*

5

Skylights, decks, courtyards, large trees, and walkways all beckon the occupant to participate in the outdoors. Such outdoor enjoyment is definitely a priority in California, as is the use of the common pool provided on the grounds of the project. Outdoor living is greatly enhanced by the expressive use of tile trim, chimney caps, and wood detailing. On the lower commercial level, ornamental storefronts also add a layer of separate focus and detail.

On the largest scale, earth-mounded plantings, varied roof heights, and slipped-wall massing create a responsive formal progression. All these elements weave humanity, architecture, and nature into a varied experience, rich in positive interaction.

EFFICIENCY

The terraces and trellises, mentioned earlier, provide a great deal of shade, aiding in the prevention of overheating. The small mass of the project's units greatly limits energy costs.

7

8

Figure 7 *Residential terrace. Set above the commercial level, a sense of privacy and local community is fostered by the common palette of materials, beveling geometries, and focal planter. Set at an elevated level, the defining units are only two stories tall, giving the space a lighter enclosure than the commercial courtyard.*

Figure 8 *Commercial courtyard. Layers of facade elements distinguish levels of use, soften facades, and yet effectively allow all units to take advantage of the air, light, and ambience of this kinetically defined space. Note how various building parts enliven the space and allow local foci to be created.*

Photographs Courtesy of the Architect

Senior Citizen

We can create great architecture, build against great odds, and profit where adversity seemed triumphant, but we will all still grow older. The percentage of our population that can be classified as senior citizens is increasing dramatically every year. It is one of the great ironies of American development that we encourage middle-aged, successful families to buy bulky, demanding homes a seeming instant before the kids leave and the parents' backs fail.

The aging of our population is providing new markets for developers. Their architects are studying the special needs of this growing market. They find that older people are fiercely proud and independent, yet experiencing new needs, vulnerabilities, and frustrations. They can no longer maintain the homes they now live in. Taxes that seemed reasonable in a full-income era now seem astronomical. Space that seemed a necessity is now visited only by dust.

The attached house is an ideal response. In joint ownership with others, maintenance can be contracted, expenses shared, and security increased. A "community" is created that can ameliorate the loneliness caused by the departure of children or the death of a spouse. Moreover, the individual home can be smaller, more efficient, and more affordable, particularly when common gathering areas are provided.

Independent, Community Living in a Rural Setting

ANNIE MAXIM HOUSE

Rochester, Massachusetts

KJA Architects

OBJECTIVES

A commanding concern of the past decade has been the aging of the nation's population. By 1985, 11 million Americans were living alone and were over the age of 55. Further, demographers predicted that during the second half of the eighties, nearly 4 million additional Americans would be in the 65-and-over age group.

While most publications on residential building challenge the industry to respond to this need, only a few architects seem to have studied gerontology at all. Fewer still seemed to have grasped what it means to provide the right kind of housing for older Americans. The associates of KJA Architects, of Cambridge, Massachusetts, have attempted to fulfill this need. Their Annie Maxim House project shows how site, building, budget, and human need can be artfully harmonized.

At first, the circumstances surrounding this project seem to defy its service as a model. It is heavily endowed by the estate of the cranberry magnate, George A. Cowen. The building is sited on 200 acres of scenic rural countryside. It overlooks an attractive pond and is set back, far from the disturbance of passing traffic. Finally, it was relatively unencumbered by governmental regulation.

Yet, it is replete with valuable lessons for housing the elderly. Success in this particular market means addressing the needs of households who are vulnerable, yet fiercely independent; living on limited resources, yet proud of their ability to take care of themselves; and strong-willed, yet fearful of change. KJA designed to resolve these dilemmas.

In addition, the architects worked on a limited budget, and built within it. They created a space that provides independence, yet encourages casual, spontane-

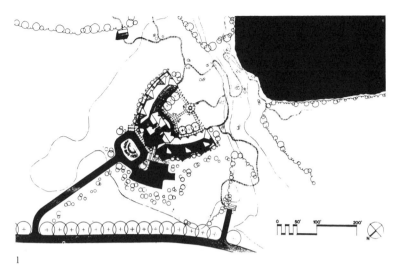

Figure 1 *Site plan. The horseshoe is focused on the inlet of a lake. Note how few parking spaces need to be facilitated in a congregate living situation.*

Figure 2 *Distant-entry prospect. The crowning hub of the convex form centers the building's overall form, providing a much-needed focal point.*

1

ous contact. They built at under $90 per square foot in 1983, which is affordable by most standards. Their carefully crafted residential environment could work in a more urban setting, where security is a paramount concern.

Affordability was assured at Annie Maxim by the endowment of the Cowen estate. Residents are not required to pay rent. Despite this luxury, residents do offer voluntary stipends, which are used by their residential community for charitable programs. The architect was, nonetheless, required to respect a modest construction budget.

It did so in several ways. First, it employed a building which creates a community setting by forming an arch, oriented toward the pond, containing individual living units that are essentially rectangular and thus cost-efficient. Second, the unit size is small, and therefore affordable, at 550 square feet. This smallness is mitigated by the completeness of the units—each has a separate bedroom, eat-in kitchen, and living room—and by the tremendous amenity of the common spaces, which draw residents from their private spaces into communal areas, blending privacy and sociability. Third, great attention is paid to energy efficiency; this is abetted by slab-on-grade construction, which also reduces construction costs. Design-enhanced cross ventilation eliminates the need for air conditioning. Fourth, relatively standard structural systems are employed; a simple, one-story wood-frame structure is built on concrete and employs 2 by 6 wood-frame walls, wood truss roof, and a post-and-beam porch. Finally, the attached-housing format greatly enhances affordability through the use of common walls and significantly reduced linear footage of infrastructure: water, walks, electrical distribution, and the like.

The needs of the resident elderly are further met by careful interior design. Corridors, alcoves, porches and common areas encourage, without forcing, social contact. Completely independent living areas allow privacy. The semiprivate interior spaces, cooking and dining, are oriented toward a common corridor, while private living and bedroom spaces are oriented toward small, private backyards. A small support staff carefully complements what the residents can do for themselves. Dignity is preserved, yet needs are met.

COMMUNITY

Annie Maxim House is relatively isolated in a rural environment. Its architecture suggests a magnificent country inn, the kind of delightful surprise one would expect, and hope, to encounter on a country road. The building seeks to recall traditional local and regional New England character through the use of porches, windows, siding and trim materials, a widow's walk, and the design of the roof.

Despite this mass, the individual units recall customary residential conventions: the kitchen overlooks a porch, with an expansive view of the outside. A picket fence borders a private backyard for each residence. Footpaths into the woods and private and community gardens further communicate a rural setting.

The surrounding acreage, most of it heavily wooded, buffers the community from surrounding communities, most of which are scattered, small, and isolated themselves. Access to the building is, of course, by car. Vehicles approach the site via a cedar-lined lane, through a 10-acre hay field, which accentuates the rural aspect of the project.

ENVIRONMENT

At 16 acres per dwelling unit, Annie Maxim House is a pillar of environmental conservation. The project evolved out of rather unique circumstances, in this regard, but provides great encouragement for land trusts, which can be used in rural, suburban, or urban settings. For example, in rapidly suburbanizing areas where farm land is threatened, community land trusts are being organized to accept donations of, or to purchase, sensitive land. These trusts often survive, financially, by developing a portion of the land acquired, but always in tastefully appropriate ways. Annie Maxim House gracefully demonstrates how environmental conservation and low-intensity development can coexist.

All the large, mature trees were retained. Vegetation in the fields and forest was preserved. Wild flowers were added to enhance the natural ambience. Parking is centralized; only one-and-a-half spaces per dwelling unit are required for the population. Impervious coverage is minimized in this way and by the small size of the individual units and the use of a gravel drive around one side of the building. The large pond at the southern end of the site is accessed by footpaths only and thus is largely preserved in its natural setting.

The building's orientation is largely dictated by the environment. The building cups toward the pond, and is designed around that view. The interior courtyard is contained by the cup, windows are placed to capture the winter sun, and porches are overhung to protect from the sun in summer. Subsoil conditions greatly influenced design. The building was raised to avoid groundwater problems. These conditions prevented basements and may have prevented multistory construction, even if desired.

Annie Maxim House is visible from a long distance: on one side from the end of the 700-foot-long hay field, and on the other from a causeway bisecting the lake. The choice of colors and the general massing including tall features, such as stacks and a cupola, were designed with the long view in mind.

ORGANIZATION

Twelve units of housing, even with common living areas, can be a rather massive structure, especially to those who have spent a lifetime in a freestanding single-family home. The architects recognized the possibility that the massing of this building could intimidate its occupants. Consequently, the design uses a horseshoe shape to limit the sense of overwhelming size. The architects further break down the project's massing by the articulation of individual units set within the arcing mass. Although the occupants needed all spaces to be set on one level, the potential for a dwelling that is too attenuated is also minimized by the building's shape.

The brilliance of this organization is not simply in its reduction of the perceived mass. In creating the distinctive arc of organization, the architects saw the potential for a crown, or, in their words, a "keystone" to the curved massing.

As interpreted by KJA, this "head" at the center point of the two wings of living units plays many roles. It serves as entry, social gathering place, and dining hall. It also provides a common kitchen, laundry, mailbox, and telephone area. Its public convex face serves as a waiting area for visitors, and its inside face has a large covered porch area facing the private view. The sense of "front porch" and "back-yard" is reinforced by this central crossroads. It is important to note that the only truly curved (and thus most expensive) walls in the entire project occur at the front entry and opposing back-side exit, allowing a proud front door and view-embracing dining area to be linked across the intervening public spaces housed at the central crossroads.

It is the nature of this crown as a dominant focal element which makes the image of this project aesthetically powerful *and* functionally appropriate. A meandering curve without a recognized single point of entry simply denies its greater sense of community.

Beyond the recognition of function and focus, the organization of this project

3

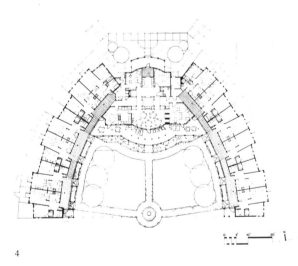

4

5

gains greater impact when the nature of the individual units is investigated. These "bricks" to the center's keystone structure are each rectilinear constructions, save one wall.

That one wall, set between each pair of mirrored units, creates the sense of curve that belies the simplicity of the plan's true layout. Since the units mirror one another, like functions always touch—bedroom to bedroom, living room to living room, etc. By creating one skewed wall as the angle bisector to each interface of angled paired units, the architect has enabled all other walls to be at right angles to one another, greatly reducing construction cost.

The clarity of the layout is carried through to the exterior faces each wing presents. At the concave side, a continuous enclosed hallway addresses the defined courtyard or backyard. On the outside wall, the units address the site with yards defined by small picket fences, providing personal outdoor space, to complement the common courtyard space. Living spaces are projected outward into these spaces, gaining corner glazing, while bath spaces project into the courtyard side hallway, defining the entry to each unit. By orienting the expansive living areas to the opening outer edge of the radial planning scheme and baths to the narrowing inner side of the fanning organization, the architects have located the spaces to respect both geometry and function.

Pulling back from these clear principles of organization, the project's massing is a marvelous recognition of a site's latent potential to give any building meaning.

Figure 3 *Courtyard. The concave aspect of the building both defines space between its wings and provides a formal focus on the lake beyond.*

Figure 4 *Plan. A horseshoe with entry at the top, and public spaces at center. Note the continuous walk, corridor, and spanning porch.*

Figure 5 *Public areas/exterior. A proud gable receives the wings, and a covered porch extends the interior space. Note the Victorian detailing.*

6

Figure 6 *Entry. A proud gable projects into the walkway, both beckoning the visitor and announcing its presence. Note the decorative rail above the porch.*

A building can be set upon a site, as an object dominating its context. Or it can respond to the site and orient itself to embrace its natural context. Not surprisingly, the Annie Maxim House does both, each response a result of its massing and organization.

Since it is a symmetrical arc of construction crowned at its center, this building presents a clearly dominant object set upon the landscape. Once the building is entered, the dominant role of the landscape, seen through the curved outer walls, is revealed, as the arc's open end is oriented to the existing pond. The massing uses familiar roof forms to create continuity in the wings' shape and define focal points at the center keystone and for each unit as gable faces.

Clarity is not necessarily found in predictable solutions, and personalization is not inherently rooted in ragged assertions. Care and creativity can provide delightful organization where symmetry might override all attempts at subtlety. The architect avoided the predictable "big house" image, and as a result, the scale of a twelve-unit project can be recognized. Because the design rejects an arbitrary massing differentiation, the building maintains a sense of identity. The Annie Maxim House conveys a depth of design rarely seen in this genre of building.

INTERIORS, AMENITIES, AND SERVICES

It is important to recognize the nature of this building's inhabitants when addressing the amenities provided in this design. Twelve units are designed to accommodate a maximum of twenty elderly people. The occupants are self-sufficient, but share at least one meal together every day. Because of this mixed functional perspective of living together while maintaining individual dignity and autonomy, the Annie Maxim House presents some thoughtful approaches to the task of community building.

Individuality is recognized by the separate kitchen, bath, and living rooms for each of the twelve separate units. But the resolve to create a sense of community is recognized in the space dedicated to common cooking, eating, and living areas. One unit is given over to a staff person, and there are shared mail, entry, and parking accommodations.

Perhaps the most extraordinary aspect of this spatial division into public and private areas is the nature of the common circulation spaces. In a standard attached-housing project for the general population, each front door has little or no shared circulation space and even less shared interior space devoted to circulation. In the effort to get self-sufficient people to share their lives without compromising their individual lifestyles, the architects created broad, single-loaded hallways focused on the inner courtyard. Beyond these enclosed hallways is an inner-ring walkway, connected to the inner hall via double doors opposite each unit's front door.

By providing a generous accommodation of casual contact, the architects have encouraged socializing. By creating a direct path to the common courtyard (both visual and in terms of access), they allowed for effortless use of this very inviting space.

All circulation leads to the common spaces at the crown of the arc, but rather than create a stiffly focused central hall, the architects have afforded the occupants several options for shared activity. There is a formal living area with fireplace facing the common courtyard, a separate library space facing away from the courtyard for more secluded activity, and a generous informal dining area within the common kitchen allowing for the most informal get-togethers. The largest space in the entire building is the one single activity space in the project, the common dining room, located at the central position of the building's keystone, with a commanding view

7

Figure 7 *View out. This photo, taken through a door, reveals the quiet sense of community the interior courtyard provides from within the building.*

of the courtyard. By providing options, the design allows for personal diversity while encouraging interaction.

The most sensitive accommodation of communal sensibility is a broad, wide back porch, half under an overhang, half fully exposed. Its length and breadth allow for several simultaneous groupings to occur, allowing for interaction, but not imposing it. The expanse of this porch extends between the wings of housing units, serving both as a bridge and as a distinct space addressing the common courtyard.

In addition to the social programming of the building, the architectural detailing is extraordinary for an attached-housing project. Farmhouse detailing is provided in both intimate and large-scale gestures. Trim work, porch detailing, and gardens are used to create a human scale in a large building. A crowning cupola, large-scale roof vents, and extended eaves work in proportion with the mass of the structure to give it a residential sensibility. Colors are both playful and familiar. In short, the detailing of the structure harbors a sense of "home," while recognizing the undeniable size of the building as a whole.

There is a shuttle bus service for shopping and social visits, and all lawn and gardening is taken care of by the project management.

In addressing so many potential needs, this project evidences the very best in accommodative shared living. The building neither forces communality nor discourages it. As residents come and go, the variety of spaces can continually adapt to the changing complexion of the small community. As with other aspects of this project, extraordinary care has been given to the nature of the amenities provided, allowing for complex social and aesthetic issues to be resolved in a powerful and positive building.

EFFICIENCY

A simple building shape can have disastrous environmental consequences. The United Nations Building in New York City is a simple slab whose east-west broadface orientation has created bizarre problems of overheating at all times of the year. If the architects forgot that an arcing horseshoe shape could prevent wind and sun from entering half of the building at any given moment, similar insolvable consequences would result.

But, as with many other aspects of the design of the Annie Maxim House, KJA used distinctive massing and detailing to further enhance the benefits given to occupants in the area of energy efficiency. The central courtyard faces south, allowing the crowning central public areas to receive the low-angle winter sun, while utilizing the public porch overhang to prevent unwanted summer solar gain.

By using a slab-on-grade method of construction, the sun captured in winter months can transfer its latent heat into the ceramic tiling of the southerly public spaces, storing it for nighttime radiation back into the building. The floor slab is shaded by the extended overhang in summer, providing a cooling masonry mass at the core of the building. The building is also heavily insulated and thoroughly sealed against unwanted infiltration of outside air.

Most ingeniously, this building uses its shape, orientation, and eaves to collect the cooling winds that waft across the lake, which serves as the focal view of the courtyard. In making use of the natural thermal flywheel of the lake's mass, the design of the building mitigates the need for summer cooling. All major spaces have generous openings to the sun, obviating the need for excessive artificial illumination.

Traditional American residential architecture often uses pronounced eaves and porch overhangs. More than simply aesthetic stylizing, overhangs prevent a great deal of wear and tear on siding, windows, and doors by preventing rain and snow from invading places where they can do a great deal of damage. Often architects try to fool mother nature with synthetic materials to prevent decay. Unfortunately, the sun and water can work in tandem to undermine almost any material typically used in moderate budget building. It is wise to use geometry to shield, rather than material to confront, the natural elements.

This building utilizes fundamental and proven methods of energy conservation in an imaginative building form, once again gleaning the best of several worlds of design criteria.

8

Figure 8 *Public spaces. Entry is to the left, living is to the right, with the common hall in between. Note the materials and detailing that create a noninstitutional ambience.*

Photographs by Steve Rosenthal

A Solar, Affordable Village

ROOSEVELT SENIOR CITIZEN HOUSING
Roosevelt, New Jersey
Kelbaugh & Lee, *Architects*

OBJECTIVES

The year 1984 was an ideal time for architects to complete an energy-efficient, affordable community for senior citizens using federal housing subsidies. A decade earlier, Congress passed the historic Housing and Community Development Act which memorialized a radical change in federal urban and housing policy. That act phased out urban renewal and a host of housing subsidy programs. In their place, it created a block-grant funding program for local community development, and the deepest, most flexible housing subsidy program yet established by the federal government.

This initiative, clumsily dubbed the Section 8 Program after its federal code section number, supplements the rents that lower-income households can reasonably afford with an amount sufficient to cover the entire cost of a project. Section 8 carries with it maximum rent limits and minimum property standards, which are serious constraints to the size, amenities, and design of assisted projects. The federal government reluctantly allows projects to utilize the upper ranges of the Section 8 rent limits, and only in compelling cases.

Kelbaugh & Lee presented a compelling case with its Roosevelt, New Jersey, project. First, they proposed designing a state-of-the-art solar energy project. Second, they promised the creation of an English-style village to enhance a community of undistinguished architecture. Third, they proposed a sensitive workable community for retired senior citizens that would enable them to live out their years comfortably, affordably, independently, and with dignity. These arguments convinced federal bureaucrats to allow the project to be built at the upper limits of cost permitted by the law. The result now seems clearly worth the expenditure.

1

Figure 1 *Entry view/major axis. Facing south, the long entry axis bypasses the "church" unit and serves to define several subspaces left and right between the unit blocks.*

Figure 2 *Site. Nine blocks of units create thresholds, axes, focal points, and spaces while rigidly orienting to an orthogonal organizing geometry. The central block is multistory, joined to a paved court, and it orients the two major axes. This unit becomes a "church" to the "town" of units. A perimeter fence defines the site boundary, while a system of paths reinforces axial relationships and helps define spaces. This site plan is drawn to reveal unit interiors.*

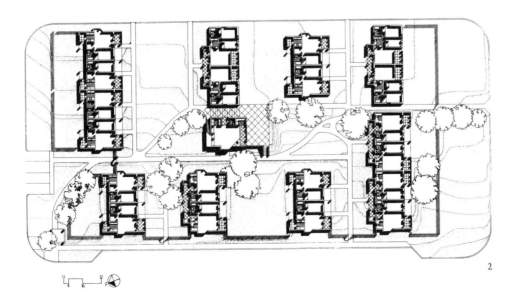

2

The borough of Roosevelt, a rural community, was settled in the 1940s, under a federally sponsored resettlement program which enabled Jewish garment-district workers to move from Brooklyn. Their houses were essentially simple concrete-block rectangles, which the owners spent decades remodeling and enhancing into typical, uninspired suburban homes. The architects captured the unsatisfied desires of these now-retiring seniors by creating a self-contained village of architectural distinction. They built twenty-one rental apartments in eight building blocks that were artfully arranged on an open site. The majority of the units were one-bedroom flats; one was a studio designed for a caretaker who would look after the property and the residents.

The 2-acre site is within walking distance of all available shopping and conveniences. Roosevelt's 600 residents all live along a block-long main road. This pedestrian orientation is carried into the development itself, which is organized around a quiet interior court devoid of vehicles—the vehicles are parked on the perimeter. In the center is a cathedral-like, three-story building which contains the caretaker's studio. The courtyard "commons," the central "church," and the low-density "cottages" on the perimeter are used to create an "English village."

Affordability is enhanced by the density of the development and the energy-efficient design. The creative passive solar techniques utilized by the architects greatly enhance the ongoing affordability of the housing by reducing heating and air conditioning costs, a critical component of an older person's budget. At ten units to the acre, the development is built at a density level that is needed to distribute land costs efficiently.

Without the benefit of federal subsidies, other New Jersey communities are creating lower-income housing, under court order, by rezoning land to this level of density. Although the federal government is still funding some senior citizen development under the Section 8 Program, the level of effort has been drastically reduced since the early 1980s. As a result, local governments are using increases in density, energy-conserving design, more minimal state subsidies, and a host of other initiatives to create affordable housing for seniors and other needy population groups. In several respects, most notably its design and its sensitivity to local needs and preferences, the Roosevelt project will remain an enduring model for these efforts, despite the withering of the federal subsidy program that made it possible.

COMMUNITY

Kelbaugh & Lee interviewed older residents of the borough before they designed this retirement village. In that process, they learned not only about the dissatisfaction with the current architecture, but much about the details of the accommodations needed for retirement. This use of "focus groups" to assist architects in designing for the specific needs of special populations is growing and is enabling architects to respond successfully to those needs.

The result in Roosevelt is a full-blown response to a community concern about the livability of the borough. There were no cherished architectural themes evident in the area around which the development could be designed. So, quite simply, the architects, with encouragement from the community, set about creating one.

ENVIRONMENT

It was the sensitivity of the federal government to oil prices and their impact on the balance of trade that led to energy auditing of most federally assisted development in the late 1970s and early 1980s. These forces were also largely responsible for the government's willingness to subsidize this project so deeply. The apartments are all oriented to the south, and heavily glazed on that side, to enable the passive solar system used by Kelbaugh & Lee to work. The last section of this article outlines the specific design approach of the architects.

With oil prices at less than half the level of the early 1980s, the federal concern with reduced energy consumption has lessened. Buildings built today will likely confront similar oil price escalation at some time during their useful lives. The Roosevelt project was the fortunate beneficiary of the heightened concern for conservation at the time. Its residents will enjoy a lifetime of savings as a result.

ORGANIZATION

Three dominant influences shaped the design of the Roosevelt Senior Citizen Housing project:

1. *Passive Solar Design.* The location of the units, their interior organization and the depth of the blocks of units were all determined by the principle of solar accessibility designed to reduce heating costs. The secondary system of passive cooling by shade and wind dictated that the existing mature trees be saved.

2. *Design Criteria for Senior Citizens.* The project responds to the occupant's need for all types of function and single-level accessibility.

3. *English Village Imagery.* The exterior scale, materials, and detailing of the project all pay homage to an English arts-and-crafts aesthetic. Never slavish, always fresh, this charming pallet of materials and their applications help coordinate the project's various buildings.

The first criterion will be discussed in depth further on, but it should be mentioned here that the solar design had a singular impact on the site plan and on the organization of the unit block massing. Buildings are kept low in height and shallow in depth to facilitate the sun's access between the project's blocks. All long block orientations are in the east-west axis to create the elongated southern exposure essential for viable solar heating. The site cooperates in the effort to use the sun by providing a benign west-northwest slope and no surrounding hills or forestation which might preempt solar utility. Nine blocks of units are thus organized, with their short ends aligned with the east and west site boundaries.

The architects then created two long circulation axes, neither completely bisecting the site, but both encountering a central vertically massed block, which is set, churchlike, at the site's center. Both axial paths orient the inside short sides of the unit blocks. At the north and south site lines, two pairs of blocks create entry thresholds for the axial paths. To the north, the blocks are slipped—the west block is moved to the south to align its north wall with the south wall of the east block. A forecourt is created, and existing trees are avoided. Kelbaugh & Lee further defined this entry condition by creating a trellis entry wall and arch between these units. The south duet of blocks have their forms aligned, creating a pierced-wall threshold for the second major axis. Secondary paths, thresholds, and axes, oriented on the north-south axis, create individual unit access. All parking is relegated to the site perimeter, creating a quiet inner world.

The arrangement of the unit blocks creates three major spaces and five minor spaces. By connecting the north, south, and west blocks with a picket fence, three additional private "backyard" spaces are created.

It should be noted that subtle manipulations of an orthogonal ordering geometry can create spatial variety, without the inherent distortions of a more arbitrary ordering system. Architecturally, eight of the nine units are quite similar in mass, material, and detail. The northeast and southwest blocks are attenuated, but all of these eight perimeter units use common eave lines, roof pitches, entry details, and glazing patterns to create a small sea of unifying building techniques, despite five slight variants of unit combination. As mentioned, amid all this consistency, one block has its two units stacked vertically. The one nonelderly resident, the caretaker, lives on the upper level. The architects thus create a central vertical focus, organizing all entrance orientation and internal circulation about a common point in reference. This "church" serves to mediate a contour shift. In the case of this unit, aberrant roof pitch, glazing patterns, and a four-sided facade design complement the vertical form to conscientiously differentiate its identity from the surrounding blocks. The two major courtyards pay homage to its form, and the "village" design criterion is well served by its presence as a small-scale hierarchical feature.

3

Figure 3 *South elevation. Sun spaces and shade porches are part of the back "facades" of these unit blocks. Note the shading technology and the ventilators employed.*

Figure 4 *"Church." Though not a public building this double unit (top floor occupied by resident staff) is the only multistory block in the project, and is meshed with the only paved public space to make a piazza-campanile focal point set at a crucial topographic level change. Note its relatively crystalline form versus the extruded nature of the surrounding single-story units.*

Figure 5 *Subaxis. Entries to north-facing units spawn paths feeding off of this easterly ascendant cross axis. Note the trellis gateway and relatively mature trees.*

4

5

INTERIORS, AMENITIES, AND SERVICES

As mentioned, the unit interiors are controlled and ordered by the orientation of "served" (bedroom, living-dining) spaces to the sun, while "serving" spaces (entry, bath, kitchen, and storage) are relegated to the northerly side of the plan. Additionally, sun spaces are added to the usable area of the living-dining area. Entry and backyard areas have sun-shielding overhangs which are air locks.

Kitchens are minimal, baths simple, and the areas of the units are limited. Amenity for seniors is best described in terms of convenience. Grade-level living, walk-to-town proximity, and a secure and well-developed site facilitate an easy lifestyle. As will be described, glazing orientations provide bright winter sun and allow summer breezes to permeate the unit's interiors. Warmth in winter, comfort in summer are amenities that occupants of any age can appreciate.

EFFICIENCY

This project is a model of passive solar heating, shading, and air-flow cooling techniques. Beyond simple southerly orientation, this project implements rigorous air-movement-controlling devices. Air locks limit air filtration. Trombe walls absorb and radiate winter solar energy while acting as heat sinks during the summer months, when they are in shade. The central roof ridge has passive ventilators which allow summer breezes to literally suck overheated air out of the unit interiors. In winter the heated air is reused by the individual heating plants, located in attic spaces.

Solar controls include the expressive sunshades over the sun spaces, the overhangs, and the deep layer of sun spaces to the south which prevent direct solar gain

Figure 6 *Unit block. A typical duet of mirrored units, where serving spaces are oriented to north (top) and served spaces face south, address a layer of outdoor-oriented spaces—sun spaces to the outside edge, covered porches to the inside. Similarly, bedrooms share a common wall, as do baths. Living spaces are located to the outside wall and benefit from the applied bay.*

Figure 7 *Typical east end. A minor southerly bay extension is attached to a blank gable end of a typical unit block. Note the solar-charged air ventilator with its glazed and framed wood housing. A crescent retaining well (foreground) and exterior light fixture (centered below ventilator) provide another light layer of elements that quietly enhance a simple elevation.*

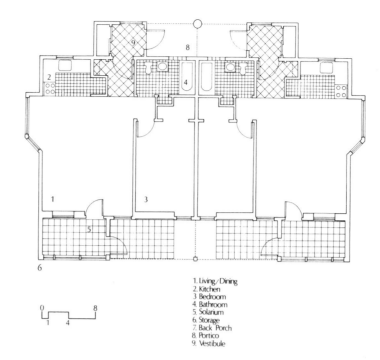

1. Living/Dining
2. Kitchen
3. Bedroom
4. Bathroom
5. Solarium
6. Storage
7. Back Porch
8. Portico
9. Vestibule

0   8
1   4

7

95

into the main living areas. The existing deciduous trees form a natural shade barrier to the summer sun.

The units are built upon concrete slab foundations, which serve as a large-scale thermal flywheel, absorbing the winter sun's energy, while radiating the earth's cooling influence in summer.

Common sense combines with common shapes and materials to create a project of uncommon resourcefulness. In coupling the needs of the elderly with the undeniable truths of energy efficiency, two rights have made a transcendant right —a project of affordable, dignified accommodation.

Figure 9 *Sections. Winter (left), summer (right)—top, through-entry; bottom, through-bedroom and bath—show a simple use of sun to heat and of airflow to cool. Both tools involve insulation, shading, absorption, and radiation of energy.*

Photographs by Otto Baitz

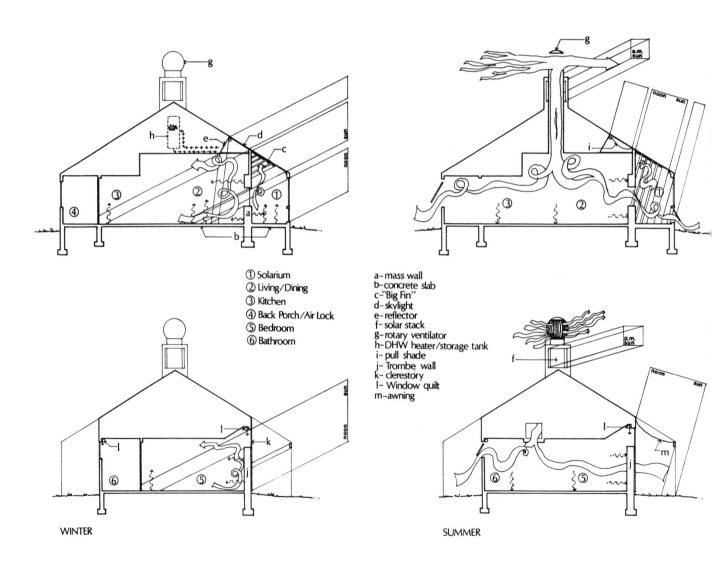

① Solarium
② Living/Dining
③ Kitchen
④ Back Porch/Air Lock
⑤ Bedroom
⑥ Bathroom

a—mass wall
b—concrete slab
c—"Big Fin"
d—skylight
e—reflector
f—solar stack
g—rotary ventilator
h—DHW heater/storage tank
i—pull shade
j—Trombe wall
k—clerestory
l—Window quilt
m—awning

WINTER

SUMMER

Recreational

The design requirements of the second home are both limiting and liberating. Often, the seasonal short-term use and enticing outdoor conditions conspire to minimize the interior design criteria "wish list." Yet, such homes must create an impression that endures through the off-season and reminds their owners of the joy of returning.

In this section, two projects by the same architect are visited. William Turnbull created two Colorado ski-oriented projects which worship views, become expressive features in the overall landscape, and facilitate a sense of hearth and home for the residents.

A Place of Places, Complementing the Mountainous Landscape

THE CENTENNIAL
Beaver Creek, Colorado
William Turnbull Associates, *Architects*

OBJECTIVES

William Turnbull set out to create an up-scale mountain retreat on a very difficult site in the newly developed ski community of Beaver Creek, Colorado. The challenges were many. First, the three-quarter-acre site had to accommodate twenty-nine residential units, a density of thirty-six units per acre. Second, development had to occur on a finger-shaped steep site. Third, it needed to blend into the natural surroundings of aspen trees, rocks, and mountainous terrain. Fourth, it had to meet the rigorous design standards of the community of Beaver Creek, which regulated siting, roof style and pitch, exterior materials, window choice, building lines, and the proportionality of building parts, as well as more traditional area and building volume and siting requirements. Fifth, it had to sell at very high prices to a choosy group of second-home buyers.

The architects specifically intended to work in the context of their natural situation. The result is an organic form patterned after the gentle and varied long-view lines of the nearby mountains. The building rises from a two-story height on the south to a seven-story "peak" and falls as it moves north to five stories, interacting with the foothills and peaks on the horizon. The natural vertical lines created by dramatic white-barked aspens and dark spruces are echoed in the building by chimney stacks, balcony lines, and window placement. Three stories are below grade through the uphill eastern portion of the site, providing space for thirty cars and storage areas for the residents.

The understated, natural lines of the building's mass are in stark contrast to its dramatic and varied interior. Units open up onto a common interior space illuminated by a four-story atrium lobby which is crossed by bridges. The emphasis

1

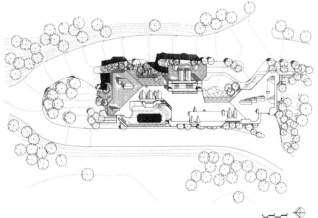

2

Figure 1 *West exposure. An evolving, ascending form is both expressive and cogent. Its mass is in scale with its natural context, while its detailing is in scale with a residential project.*

Figure 2 *Site. A Y intersection, set upon a steep incline has its oddball outline filled with building and building-defined spaces. Two courts are created: upper-right for vehicular access and center for public focus and gathering. Lower-right access is for service and parking.*

from within the individual units is on exterior views of Grouse Mountain, Beaver Creek Valley, and the McCoy Mountain ridgeline.

The amenities of these condominium units, the views, the comfortable communication of interior spaces, and the natural fit of the building met the test of the market. Units sold from over a quarter-million dollars to in excess of a million dollars in the mid-1980s. The design also met the rigorous and varied local architectural regulations, which had the intended result of tying the building into the village center as well as the surrounding environment.

COMMUNITY AND ENVIRONMENT

What the architects did with the design of The Centennial is a microcosm of the master design of Beaver Creek, which demands continuity of expression between the built and natural environments. The architectural theme for the community, as expressed in its Architectural Guidelines, is "to establish a remote village with its own identity, a place of places, complementing rather than competing with the natural landscape." The guidelines call for an understated long view with "exciting vitality and broad individual expression" in the center.

Consistent with these requirements, the architects used glazed clay tiles on the roof and stucco exterior walls with cedar trim, railings, and decks—all natural materials that integrated the building into the environment. These details reinforced the effect of the lines of the building's mass to tie the building into the seamless blend of building, vegetation, and terrain in the spirit of the overall Beaver Creek design.

ORGANIZATION

How much "organization" can a twenty-nine-unit project impose on a 0.789-acre site? Under the thoughtful hands of the architects, and the equally focused attention of the Beaver Creek zoning regulations, the result was a dramatically expressive building which has a definite control over its site.

Few sites are as difficult to build on as this: small, bounded on two sides by roads which converge to form a fork at one side of the site—a veritable "finger" of property. Compounding the lot's problematic shape, its contours drop two full stories across the *short* dimension of the site. Further, its long dimension faces west, not toward the southern exposure best suited to the brutal cold encountered in Beaver Creek.

Despite these natural obstacles, the building responds to virtually all the zoning criteria and site limitations. The resulting structure organizes the twenty-nine units with several bold planning decisions. First and foremost, a central "street" is created within the building envelope, which opens up to a six-story atrium common area at the middle of the plan. This spine of space links all elements of the project and divides the interior into three distinct wings—north, south, and west. Stairs meander within this interstitial area, creating a sense of adventurous level changes.

In creating a central locus for the entire project in the form of a common spatial experience, the architects have given the project a coherent internal identity. Similarly, the exterior of the project has a singular, though variegated, form. This mutational form is the direct result of several design criteria. As discussed, the site's shape and contours had a severe limit on the project's footprint and interior layout.

Secondly, the thoughtful and complete zoning ordinances of Beaver Creek determined roof pitch and form, quantity of glazing, essential formal characteristics, and even exterior material specifications. Third, the project's functional requirements essentially dictated that a multistory, high-density project had to be built.

The three unit clusters within the building's overall form are substructures, with their own column grid and simple span steel-bar joists. This orthogonal pattern is complemented by a secondary 45° diagonal geometry of plan extensions and permutations.

Beyond these rudimentary organizing features, there are four interwoven large-scale components to this project's organization. The slope of the site preordained that parking be relegated to the underground east side of the lowest level. The internal room layout is primarily determined by the aforementioned "spine." But at a smaller scale the idiosyncratic imperative evidenced in the formal manipulations can be seen in the nearly unique design each unit has. Lastly the slope's impact, the spine's organization, and individual unit articulation have a single unifying feature: the exquisitely proportioned and detailed roof.

At once massive enough to cover twenty-nine units, the roof's form follows the mandated pitch and shape of the code. Its ascendance to a full five-story eave height amidships is counterpointed by ends that are pulled down to within two stories of grade. This middle ascent is reinforced by expressed chimney forms that, when married to window arrays, create a unified sense of internal vertical thrust, expressed externally.

Secondary applications of minor roof forms—dormers, extensions, hips, sheds, and folds—all conspire to create local centers, progressions, bands, patterns, and axes. The integration of form, facade, and roof is essential to the apprehension that this is a *designed* building, not an accidental collision of parts.

This is an organic, layered building which has local and grand articulations and movements. It is not the product of a gridded, conscious rationale, but a thoroughly conscientious effort at making the massive friendly. Its adherence to the zoning code is inventive. Its mutations are controlled, yet expressive. Its multiple unit designs are unified by the consistent spine and superimposed roof. The patterns of its meandering facade are organized by lines and centers and yet have a fresh sense of spontaneity.

In the final result, this seemingly disorganized organic form is a cogent mesh of the consistent and the spontaneous. The architects succeeded in producing life with logic.

INTERIORS, AMENITIES, AND SERVICES

This is a high-priced resort condominium of moderately sized units. It is intended for nocturnal, part-time occupancy. Therefore, its amenities are greatly enhanced by the proximity to the snow and nature that is Colorado.

All units have fireplaces. Many have cathedral ceilings. Most have decks. Each unit has a laundry. Most bedrooms have their own bath. Closets are commodious. Most units are duplexes. Many have bay windows or octagonal extensions. All have access to the unifying atrium. All materials are first-rate.

But the greatest amenity is the locale, and its presence from within and without. The glazing, the decks, and the internal unit orientation all conspire to bring cold, snowy vantages into the safe, warm confines of the home.

With part-time occupancy, and a preoccupation with nature, this is not a prototypical project in terms of its specific features. However, in its conquering of a difficult site and tight zoning guidelines, this project excels where others fail.

3

Figure 3 *Entry court. As the form descends (left) in a wing of units, the major interior space and vertical flue array is expressed (center). Windows, decks, and flues cluster, while broad expanses of blank facade provide counterpoint to the activity.*

EFFICIENCY

A southern exposure was prohibited here by the lay of the land. However, the primary view was to the west, and in a resort community, morning hours are not often spent at home. But when cold skiers come home, the setting sun has newly warmed the entire interior, utilizing the multistory atrium as a convection space. As you might expect, this post-energy-crisis building set in the frigid Rockies has maximal insulation, energy-efficient glazing, and independent heat plants for each unit.

The shallow building section helps promote maximal solar penetration and natural ventilation. The inherently compact nature of a stacked building mass also mitigates radiant cooling.

4

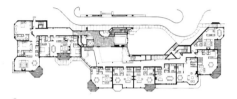

5a

5b

6

Figure 4 *West elevation. A progressive formal ascendance is counterpointed with intermittent banding of terraces and windows. Minor vertical alignments help redefine the local facade foci. Intermediate scaler devices such as the major courtyard concavity (left) help mediate between the dominant massing and the relatively miniature necessities of unit glazing and dormer articulation.*

Figure 5 *Plans,*

(a) *Entry. A central service core provides an elevator, public room, and airlock between covered front entry (top) and multistory lobby (below). Expressive stairs, curtain wall glazing, and structure create a central space which spawns two wings of single loaded corridors. Octagonal porches, plan projections, and folds soften a potentially monolithic mass.*

(b) *Upper level. The sinuous circulation services three unit concentrations and in the process spans the vertical space. Note the hallway-side serving spaces and the elongated, view-hugging served spaces.*

Figure 6 *Public space. Horizontal bands of semidetached circulation are counterpointed by vertical structure, glazing, and space. Levels communicate, and the scale of building is respected by the vertical datum of this space.*

Figure 7 *Unit interior. A triad of interacting gable dormers ascends in expressive articulation, not unlike the entire complex itself.*

Photographs by Wolfgang Herzog

7

A Doorway on the Slopes
and a View of the Valley

WOODRUN PLACE CONDOMINIUMS

Snowmass, Colorado

William Turnbull, *Architect*

OBJECTIVES

Woodrun Place is organized around a principal objective: to provide maximum access to the formidable slopes of Snowmass from the major chairlift, which is directly adjacent to the site. The building cups an octagonal plaza at the top, then undulates down the slope, imitating the course of a skier on a gentle run. From the upland plaza, one can walk down stairs and then through a pedestrian arcade along the full length of the building. This feature provides ready communication with the nearby ski areas; downstairs town house owners have direct ski-out, ski-in access. The upstairs, larger town houses enjoy commanding views of Snowmass Valley, and yet have ready access to the slopes via the arcade.

   The building houses fifty-six condominium town houses, an equal number of covered parking spaces, a recreational spa, and a conference center. It provides year-round accommodations in Snowmass, which is located just north of Aspen, itself becoming a four-season resort area. The winter season dictated the design, nonetheless, with the covered pedestrian run serving as a major cold weather amenity.

COMMUNITY AND ENVIRONMENT

Site conditions and local regulations also dictated some of the form. It was imperative to organize the building in a way that prevented shadows on adjacent roads and homes. Vehicular access was determined by a mandated fire access road through the site.

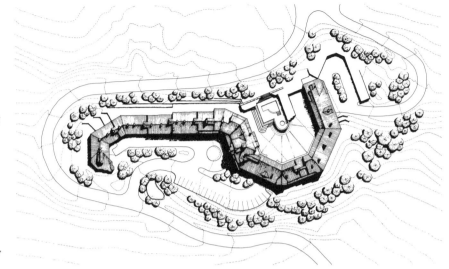

Figure 1 *Site. A meandering, stepping wall flexes, counterflexes, and configures to the existing road's twists and turns. The lower court provides access, the upper court a public focus. The right drive provides parking access.*

Figure 2 *Distant entry. As the foreground wing descends to a human scale and decomposes to express structure and animate roof, the vertically projective local center of entry beckons.*

Local governmental standards dictated variation in facade design by prohibiting the construction of a single uninterrupted building face longer than 160 feet. The undulation and articulation of the structure nicely accommodated this design standard of the community. The effect on the mountainous landscape is alluring, with the building growing naturally up the slope, lightly resembling the lines of nearby hills before they pitch toward the top of the horizon.

Local resistance to unchecked growth tempered the density proposed and, thereby, enhanced the gentleness of the building. Compared to the effect of nearby buildings that seem erratically placed on the landscape, Woodrun has an organized visual impact, lending congruity to the area.

The exterior stucco treatment was selected to match the surrounding hillsides. The site plan preserved the natural tree cover, which was enhanced with additional plantings.

ORGANIZATION

Colorado is a state of vistas. Ascendant mountains, clear skies, and open countryside present the natural world in breathtaking sweep and scale. Building a resort town house complex is an exercise in responding to that natural world. Hence, views, terrain, and access to skiing are the focal criteria in the basic organization of this project. A sinuous angling structure, this project contorts to catch vistas up, down, and across the Snowmass Valley. The building ascends the slope of the 2.3-acre site, and then its own height ascends to over six stories at the middle. What might come as a surprise to the uninformed observer is that this building is in strict compliance with tough zoning laws; it is also carefully massed to avoid casting shadows upon adjacent buildings and roads.

The expressive shape and massing harbor a variety of interior organizing features and concepts. Essentially a simple span wood-frame and steel-column structure, the entire building accommodates several circulation patterns and types. Entries are defined for both cars and people. Cars may enter at either end of the oblong site and cross it diagonally. They are parked in fully covered spaces, most relating directly to the units they serve. People enter the site from a variety of common and private access points. The spatial foci of all this circulation are the two concavities created by the counterflexing building form. A minor cupping on the downhill side of the hill receives cars and contains a narrow bay of three-story units, whose first level is for access and parking. The building's footprint straightens and returns more tightly to create an octagonal court. As the terrain rises, so does the building's mass; finally reaching a six-story height at the juncture of the two concavities, which is the initial focal point of both vehicular-entry thresholds. This central mass harbors a lobby, conference room, and stair and elevator core.

The building thus produces a "head" by utilizing the natural terrain and the rising height and widening girth of the building's form. The exterior courtyards use this formal progression to help reinforce their functional identities. The looser, more open cupping to the east is utilized predominantly as a point of site entry. The taller, more tightly coiled upper court sits above the underground parking, harbors a pool, and creates the common focus of many units as they soak up the southern sun. A bright, paved urban court, and a loose, dimmer lower court provide two distinct entries. Each is more effective because the other exists. Each focuses attention and provides circulatory distribution. Both are linked by a grade-level covered arcade, which is essential to easy access to the outside by skiers.

Roof peak lines ascend as the form climbs the slope, and the width of the building bay grows with each step up. Dormers and chimneys vary in size and are used to highlight parts of the form. Exterior screens of porches form a large-scale

3

Figure 3 *West lattice. Large-scale animation of a structural grid. Decks, steps, and minor distortions of the expressed system create a varied and evocative datum.*

Figure 4 *Entry. Elements that meander elsewhere are coalesced at this focal point to create a concerted effort at focus.*

Figure 5 *Section/axonometric. Each unit has private outside access. Upper units have cathedral spaces. Roof and structure are expressively manipulated by the exterior skin.*

5

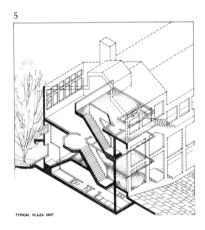

TYPICAL PLAZA UNIT

Figure 6 *Ground floor. The beveling form has units touching the ground right and center, with parking and unit-access stairs between. Central open stairs connect lower entry court (right) to upper public court with pool (center). Note the extended wing of covered parking (left).*

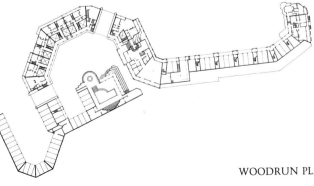

4

Figure 7 *North face. A linear form steps up the terrain, and is punctuated by light vertical projections. Windows and terraces are expressively coordinated to enhance the progression.*

Photographs Courtesy of the Architect

WOODRUN PLACE CONDOMINIUMS

107

grid-lattice across the beveling facades, creating both depth and datum. The building's width is reduced as its height increases, creating a reduced mass at its highest point and helping to reinforce some of the local centers mentioned earlier.

This is a building which weaves circulation, form, and exterior space to deal with a hillside. Set in a peninsula of earth bound on three sides by a winding road, and stepping up the site to catch views and light, the building comfortably incorporates all these design criteria in a simply conceived, relentlessly expressed form. The architect's use of surface articulation brings a large building into a scale that is comfortable for its occupants.

INTERIORS, AMENITIES, AND SERVICES

A luxury second-home condominium needs to justify its cost with more than its wonderful location. Woodrun Place holds little back in its celebration of "the good life." Each unit has a fireplace. Elevators provide access to the stacked units at the middle of the building mass. There is a significant effort to provide soundproofing between units. Top-floor accommodations all have cathedral ceilings and double-height spaces. Maid service is provided. There is a pond filled with melted snow, and a pool in the common court. There is also a lobby and conference room on the grade level, which, combined with an in-house spa, give a feeling that every need is accommodated.

But perhaps the greatest gift to its occupants is the narrow building bay which often facilitates *two* wonderful views. Most units have balconies to address these views, and individual ski-in, ski-out entries. The immediately adjacent ski lift provides instant gratification for those addicted to the slopes. Someone once said that the three rules of real estate are "location, location, location"—these golden "rules" were written for projects such as Woodrun Place.

EFFICIENCY

The existing slope fades away from the south, mitigating winter solar access. But the materials and systems used attempt to compensate for the site's limitations. A tight box, covered in stucco with a prefabricated cement tile roof, the building presents a relatively impenetrable skin. Heavy batt and rigid insulation are used throughout the project.

There is also a centralized boiler system with independent thermostats, which provides efficient heat and hot water production.

Affordable

All the projects in this book are shaped and limited by market forces. Size, shape, and texture in good projects are keyed carefully to the tastes and budgets of their intended occupants. They are even more carefully tuned by the financial players: the contributors of equity and debt financing that make the projects feasible.

In this section we evaluate projects that are financed by tightly regulated federal subsidy programs or tax-exempt bonds or by an array of innovative sources of funds, each with separate requirements. The challenge of building for low- and moderate-income households is not only the challenge of building on a budget but the architect must toe additional regulatory lines as well. For example, federally funded projects must meet the infamous "minimum property standards" and a host of noise and environmental minimums as well.

The combination of building for a captive market and complying with such spirit-deadening design limits has often resulted in dull architecture. This need not be the case, as is so graphically illustrated in the next several pages. As if to emphasize the point, our cover story is found here. Antoine Predock's neon-lighted southwestern art project in Albuquerque shows that "affordable" is not a euphemism for "cheap" or "plain" or "simple."

Design Excellence
in a Renewal District

UNIVERSITY CITY TOWNHOUSES
Philadelphia, Pennsylvania
Friday Associates, *Architects*

OBJECTIVES

In a 1976 amendment to the National Housing Act, Congress stated a clear national policy calling for "the elimination of substandard and other inadequate housing . . . and the realization as soon as feasible of the goal of a decent home and suitable living environment of every American family." This articulates the other American housing dream: that of lower-income families caught in the deepening spiral of urban poverty. That dream has grown faint as program after program has been slashed or eliminated by the federal government.

In part, the demise of such programs is due to their frequent inability to create livable communities, not to mention their hapless architecture. The forces which lobbied successfully for the withering of federal funding for inner-city development used photographs of faceless public housing buildings, plaintively awaiting the demolition crew. The failure of the developers of federally assisted housing to create a sufficient number of successful images of decent housing contributed greatly to the reversal of the commitment of Congress to its laudable goal.

University City Townhouses was constructed in 1983, the year that marked the retreat of the federal government from the urban battlefield. That irony is compounded by the magnificent success of the project's architects in creating a distinct, proud residential neighborhood in an urban renewal district. This site, like countless others over previous decades, was acquired, cleared, and served with infrastructure through the federal urban renewal process. Local renewal bonds, guaranteed by the federal government, were issued and the proceeds used to bring such sites to the point of development, often of housing, itself subsidized by one of several federal programs.

Figure 1 *Site. Eight blocks of units are organized to create public courtyards (center, right), private backyards (between double units), axial paths (center, top) and parking (upper left and right). The rhythms created are in scale with the neighborhood. Movement, site, unit entry, and various activities are all accommodated.*

Figure 2 *Streetscape. Expressed three-story gable ends march down a typical city street. Parapet wall extensions, roof, facade, and spatial variations create a coordinated personalization of scale and image.*

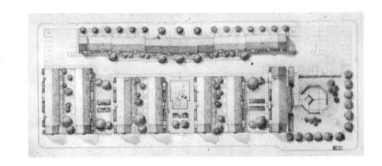

1

2

3

Figure 3 *Long unit facade. Entry and bay projections of contrasting and decorous stucco combine with brick color banding to preempt the potential for this large unit block to be a scaleless, impersonal form.*

Figure 4 *Typical bay. Art and architecture combine to create a formal element with extraordinary impact and depth. Its location is often set above doors (as in this photo) creating door protection and an entry threshold.*

By 1983, in Philadelphia, the importance of good design and a livable scale was clear to the city which sponsored a design competition for the University City site. This contest was entered and won by a local firm of distinction, Friday Associates. Among their qualifications was an intimate knowledge of local residential architecture, which they called upon to create a comfortable, well-appointed residential community. The result was criticized by some for being too luxurious for low-income housing. Its fit with the architectural motifs of West Philadelphia was unusually appropriate for any type of development.

The architects made the units affordable to low-income families while developing a well-integrated, appropriately scaled neighborhood of seventy town houses on 2.8 acres. They turned the project's back on adjacent Market Street, a commercial artery, and oriented the units toward one another creating a neighborhood of front stoop living, with interior streets, recreational areas, and backyards with patios and garden spaces.

Affordability was achieved by using varied but simple forms and by keeping materials modest without sacrificing design. The Section 8 Program of the federal government, which was used to subsidize the final costs, required compliance with certain minimum property standards. Such compliance was achieved through the

4

use of aluminum siding and stucco and brick veneer over studs: materials adaptable enough to catch the flavor of the Victorian era architecture in the neighborhood. The final costs were $42 per square foot for units averaging nearly three bedrooms per apartment, providing desperately needed housing for larger Philadelphian families.

COMMUNITY

The project achieved quick and widespread acceptance in the community. Its use of front porches, bays, brackets, patterned brick, ornamental plaster, and clapboard siding reflected Victorian tastes prevalent in the area, and belied the public nature of the project.

West Philadelphia homes, many of them row houses themselves, feature ornamental architecture and accentuated residential features such as those employed by Friday Associates. Its interior streets, community amphitheater, and residential character seem a logical extension of other existing neighborhoods. That an urban renewal "project" could so obviously take its proper place in the seamless web of domestic architecture was a pleasant surprise to the community.

ENVIRONMENT

As a vacant piece of urban renewal turf, the site has no environmental features to preserve or contend with. The site plan was designed with the idea of creating environmental amenities to complement the development's scheme. The courtyard, backyards, and private streets add some landscaping to the 2.8 acres, as do the trees planted along two busy abutting streets. One corner of the site was preserved as open space, and parking was kept to a minimum. In effect, the cozy small-scale neighborhood in the midst of a mixed-use area with high-rise buildings on one side and a commercial area on another adds a balance to the environment valuable in itself.

ORGANIZATION

Since the site is a complete city block, this scheme is organized by an orthogonal street grid. Such rectilinear organization makes simple-span bearing-wall construction quite easy to execute. The architects recognized the potential for scaleless building and space if the street defined a block building type. The hard edge of Market Street could be an impenetrable wall if followed by a multistory building. In such a scenario, the street's noise and traffic would create a decidedly unresidential character. But if the street's presence is completely denied by the orientation of the new construction, then the existing neighborhood of town houses would be effectively rejected, relegating this project into a "brave new world" of dissonant imposition. Rather than toeing the line or cutting it, the architects respected the street while obviating its problematic qualities. Blocks of units were turned at 90° to the street. Paired by connecting walls at each narrow end of the oblong blocks, each duet forms a private court in between and a public court between it and the flanking twin blocks. Three of these blocks create four internally focused courts. A minor single row of units necessitated by the site's dimensions has a corner park as its front "door." Central to these seven rows (three duets, one isolated) is a common park and playground.

This space serves several functions. It creates a community center, designed as a hub for gathering. It provides primary access for two of the duet blocks. It connects the street to the last built element of the site, a long stepped block that stretches across the back side of the site. Approximately the length of three of the single blocks in a duet unit, it faces the back street and terminates at each end at the corner parking lots, which service the entire project.

The aforementioned central gathering plaza and playground is related to the long block's center. An access street for emergency vehicles follows the inside edge of this block. All these internal spaces are essential for the sort of occupant monitoring an urban housing project needs to create a sense of security.

The sequence of spaces imposed on the site—linear, centered, corner, and courtyard—facilitates a sense of occupant comfort that no monolithic construction could hope to duplicate. In so doing, these units carry on the existing rhythms of the street's construction. As its low construction cost indicates, this level of design does not carry the inevitable pricing consequences of other features imposed on projects by some architects. It's always cheaper to build one form (as opposed to eight), but if the forms are as simple as those in this project, the costs are minimized.

To prevent the simplicity of the structures from being a boring array of buildings, the architects have imposed a secondary system of surface and formal development that unites the various units, while at the same time reinforcing individual aspects of each unit.

Figure 5 *Entry axis. The ceremonial brick gateway is oriented to a second-story ornamented bay projection across the public court.*

Figure 6 *Entry. A widened public court has a celebrational gateway set in a central position. Pediment forms are echoed in the gateway and unit entries, as well as in the bay projections and the street-facing gable ends.*

The street-side end-gable faces of each twin unit are given an extra story, forming the 10 four-bedroom units, and thus carrying on the scale of the street's existing buildings. Unit entrances, facing away from the street (as are grade-level windows) are designed to be pavilions. Entrances to the courtyards are also reinforced with simple, expressive thresholds, and those thresholds are received by facade elements which will be described in the next section.

Two tones of brick are used to further enhance the distinction between the individual blocks marching down Market Street. Bands of lighter brick are used to wrap at the base and at the second-story window sill height, further breaking down the potential for scaleless massing. The colors of roofing materials are varied to respond to these massing manipulations as well.

The next section will deal with the last level of design articulation which reinforces all of these large-scale organizing features, but it is important to note the guiding principles this scheme evidences.

1. *Scale.* The three-story gable ends mentioned earlier occur only at the street side of the duet units, leaving the main body of the units which face one another at two stories; this allows light, air, and low-density ambience to permeate the defined exterior spaces. Similarly, each unit entry has an overhead single-story covering, either an attached roof or cantilevered bay overhang, bringing the elongated row-house form into human scale at entry.

2. *Spatial Definition.* The architects organized the units to have facing entries, and alternately, facing rear yards, and in so doing reinforced the *nature* of the exterior space. By a creation of overtly public places at one corner and at the major cross axis, the design allows the character of the spaces to respond to their site condition. Since cars are relegated to two street corners, the issue of urban imposition into residential space is deftly handled, and ease of car access guaranteed.

3. *Formal Responsiveness.* Density can be achieved without a rude disruption of the existing neighborhood's character *if* innovative planning is used to provide common access, efficient parking, and selective heavy loading of units—where it can be done without violating principles 1 and 2 above. Density in this project was facilitated by the use of the elongated block at the back of the project.

Any project can benefit from a sense of scale, spatial definition, and formal responsiveness, but in a low-budget development these are crucial to enhancing the sense of amenity and community vital to a project's social survival.

INTERIORS, AMENITIES, AND SERVICES

First and foremost, this project's chief amenity is its affordability. Its location on a major thoroughfare in the heart of a major city provides easy access to work, shopping, and mass transit. The previously mentioned common park and playgrounds (central and corner) have both play space and sculpture. There is common garbage collection, and a community room is available.

The units themselves are quite small, with two bedrooms at 900 square feet, three at 1080, and four at 1345. Parking is limited to on-street spaces plus fifty off-street spaces. The interiors are spartan, low-cost, and functional.

It is in the area of ornamental articulation that this project is both visionary and rooted in the pride of place commonly referenced to an earlier era.

In the large sense, bay windows, gable-eave parapet wall extensions, and the use of multicolored brick and stucco are used to provide a rich blend of form and material. The unforgettable aspect of design enrichment in this project is the stucco work applied to local points of projected bays.

Under the guidance of artist Michael Webb—utilizing a "1 percent for art" program—ornament became an integral part of the project. An Italian-Swiss process called *sgraffito* was used. A lime mixture was applied to wet stucco, creating both color and texture changes. By using templates, the artist's exquisite design was easily reintroduced to the crucial focal bays, described earlier. Such detail work needs pinpoint construction coordination, but the effort is obviously worth it. This two-dimensional ornament has a light three-dimensional enhancement in the form of an ornamental bracket set under the bay extension, and the expressed gable-eave extension mentioned earlier.

Secondarily, the brick patterning focuses on street-facing unit gable ends to embrace the stock bay windows. The first-floor street-facing walls are windowless (helping limit street noise intrusion), and this brick ornamentalization of the bay combines with the extended-eave parapet to create a large focal point above street level.

In short, simple forms are given life with applications of surface variation and subdominant elements. By being secondary veneers or tack-on elements, these components are inherently limited in their added cost. Without them and the sensitive site design, this project would be but another "quick fix" applied to the open wound of inadequate low-income housing. With the touch of thoughtful detailing and massing, this project has become a prideful place to live, a gift to the neighborhood.

EFFICIENCY

Common-wall construction is inherently energy-efficient because it minimizes mass and surface area, limiting radiant cooling and internal air volume to be treated. High standards of insulation were used in construction, and glazing was efficient and limited.

Figure 8 *Public court. A central play sculpture and opposing first-floor covered entries and second-story bay projections help define an urban space. Note brick banding and stucco detailing.*

Photographs Courtesy of the Architects

Neon Navajo Motifs
and Tax-Exempt Financing

THE BEACH

Albuquerque, New Mexico

Antoine Predock, *Architect*

OBJECTIVES

This low-budget, high-art development provides affordable housing for its tenants and creates a distinctively southwestern image. The Beach contains seventy-four rental apartments, fifteen of which are rented to lower-income families. The remainder are leased to middle-income households. These apartments are constructed along U.S. Highway 66 in West Albuquerque. The buildings step up to four stories in height and blend a host of images that are common to the area.

The strip of land that constitutes the site for this string of apartments is the buffer between Highway 66, with its motels and cafés with their neon lights and largely Hispanic clientele, and the Albuquerque Country Club, with its exclusive fairways. Albuquerque itself has emerged from a cliff-dwelling Native American past into a high-tech commercial present.

To create its own landscape through architecture, the development uses a variety of images. The buildings zigzag along the highway frontage and step up and down along their elevation, in a pattern similar to a Navajo Indian blanket design. The coloration is reminiscent of the work of artists such as R. C. Gorman or Amado Peña, complements of the southwestern earth and sky. This motif is accentuated on the highway side by neon eave highlighting. From a distance, in the daytime, the mass is an undulating geological formation with a suggestion of cliff dwelling; at night, it is a neon-lighted, Navajo roadside presence, conjuring enduring motel and café images from a simpler past.

On the country club side a simpler form is presented. There the zigzag form is more subdued, the elevations are less varied, the colors more Mediterranean than Navajo, and the uses less active.

All this imagery and illumination highlights a project that mixes income

Figure 1 *Projections. Seen from a southerly street-side vantage, formal massing acts in concert with outside stair access to upper-level units, expressed chimney flues, painted facade patterning, and stepped neon detailing to create a thoroughly invigorated image of integrated ascendance. Minor projections, recesses, and broad planes of stucco serve to reinforce the latent sculptural quality of these focal points. Note the common parking lot at lower left.*

Figure 2 *Site. Bounded by water (top and right) and by road (bottom), a narrow lot skews unit orientation on a 45° bias to focus views on the mountains to the southeast and to aid in shading. A meandering access road slips in and out of the site, helping to create triangular entry and parking courts fronting the road. The opposite side of orientation aligning the ragged edge of the project addresses a country club.*

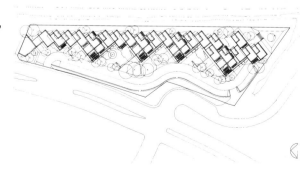

groups as well as motifs. Fifteen of the units are made affordable by the budget consciousness of the architect and developer and by virtue of low-cost tax-exempt financing. The development costs of the project were kept under $50 per square foot, a remarkable achievement for such a richly textured and intricately designed development. This was accomplished by involving the contractor from the earliest beginnings and carefully engineering all the construction details. Also, the site is fully utilized and on-site development, including parking, is kept to a minimum.

The Internal Revenue Code confers exemption from federal income taxation on bonds issued to finance rental housing projects, but only where at least 20 percent of the units are rented to lower-income households. Historically, the Congress has used the tax code to accomplish a broad range of development objectives. First among tax-advantaged real estate is the private home mortgage and property tax deduction, which slashes the real costs of owning a private home: The larger the mortgage and the greater the taxes, the more sizable the tax break—an incentive to build large and finance much. Artificially accelerated depreciation schedules for commercial and residential rental projects have long drawn investment income into market-rate rental real estate, because they create high after-tax returns. Countless other tax advantages have for years turned the business of investing in real estate into a matter of tax analysis rather than the basic economics of owning a building.

After the Tax Reform Act of 1986, many fewer tax advantages exist, and the business of real estate ownership is much more attuned to market forces. The code still gives a tax credit for the improvement of older commercial buildings and historic properties. It also provides the incentive of lower financing rates through tax exemption afforded to bonds that finance houses where 20 percent of the units are rented to lower-income households. The Beach is a contemporary example of this tax code provision put to very good effect.

COMMUNITY AND ENVIRONMENT

The architect's response to the multifaceted community and environment surrounding the site was to create this mixed-motif landscape which through architecture creates a landscape all its own. The ebb and flow of light, image, and activity along Highway 66 continues unbroken, but is highly accentuated, along the 750-foot frontage of the project. The open terrain on the country club side is complemented by the muted color and design of that side of the building. The form itself is a comfortable complement to the dramatic mountain backdrop to the west.

The response to community needs of affordable housing is most dramatic, of course, in its human dimension. The Beach affords housing for police officers, young families, single people, students, and other groups who flavor the demography of cities like Albuquerque.

ORGANIZATION

This project has almost predictable organizing features. A local stylistic context provides a basis for all the materials used and details applied. The site has its slightly awkward area filled in with units to maximize density. Several large existing trees were saved. Costs dictated many design decisions. Simple orthogonal light-frame construction regulates all the essential plan and form manipulations. These are common design determinates. Why then is this project so visually striking and innovatively organized?

This project manifests Antoine Predock's insight and spirit, which separate its design from the easy answers we see in the vast majority of similar projects cluttering the American landscape. The Beach was executed on a site that had poor subsoil conditions for under $50 per square foot, and yet it evidences the sort of innovative aesthetic exploration commonly associated with high-cost construction. The architects in turn are quick to credit the project's builder, Bradbury & Stamm Co., whose ingenuity accomplished much within the given budgetary limits. Two-coat "power-coat" stucco, flat roofs, and slab footings were invoked to save money in the middle of the design/build process. If a contractor brings a defensive or proprietary attitude into any project, the ability to manipulate the available resources is limited. Similarly, if the owner or architect has a hidden agenda and tries to subvert the contractor's legitimate attention to a fair profit, the project will ultimately suffer. The Beach is the result of a successful partnership between a resourceful architect, a focused client, and an open-minded builder.

Beyond the simple economies effected, the vision this project presents has its basis in two concerns common to many projects of far less import.

First, the site afforded an extraordinary view to the nearby Sandia Mountains—a view whose orientation is set at 45° to the datum of the primary site feature, the road along which the project is built. Secondly, the low-density surrounding neighborhood has a rather complete set of aesthetic rules and ordering devices. In concert, these two benign influences create an interwoven mass of stucco, spiced with neon (like the adjacent commercial buildings' signs) whose entire form is skewed to the view-embracing angle. The use of simple stucco surfacing, which is seen in the local architecture, helps to mesh the unprecedented formal manipulations with the local ambience. Stock paint is used in a manner familiar with the local architecture, but the specific application further amplifies the kinetic appeal of the permutational form.

The stepping form stretches 750 feet along the road and has specialized ends (a minor park and 3450 square feet of commercial rental space). This ever-cranking mass has four promontories and seven fully expressed exterior stairs to give the meandering mass local foci. Minor projections of chimney flues, rooftop terraces, stepping parapets, raised walks, and balconies further enliven the "mega form," as do small-scale perforations and voids which fleck the facades. A minimountainscape is thus created, allusive to both the adjacent environment and architecture. The ambiguous scale of the project was actually enhanced by the deletion of the tile roofs—dropped from the original plans to save money. But most evocative aspects of this project transcend its clever formal manipulations. The use of stepping neon for highlighting and strip patterning of the paint detailing mentioned earlier have a strong visual impact.

The straight back line of the site which addresses both view and some tough drainage considerations has a tighter, lower crenelated form set close to its hard edge. The main access road follows the steps of the angling front-side line with a few gentle curves. Parking is deftly handled in the triangular spaces left in the wake of the project's stepping plan. The two large cottonwood trees remain in the front-yard space, and more new trees are added to this area as an organic fringe set against the architectural manipulations.

The addressing of so many concerns, with so little evident compromise gives hope to any project. It is always expedient to eschew creativity in favor of the obvious, or conversely to assume mediocrity is implicit in linkage with the past. Money is also an excuse, unless you can overcome limits with raw innovation.

INTERIORS, AMENITIES, AND SERVICES

In affordable housing the chief amenity is in fact the ability to find new, high-art housing with a viable price tag. But this project embraces several positive site proximities. The views are wonderful and crucial to the entire project's orientation.

Figure 3 *Streetscape. Neon conspires with time-exposed headlights to create a dynamic image of movement, automotive and architectural. The interactive patterning of the facade enhances the sense of progression and detail.*

Figure 4 *Axonometric. As seen from the road-side orientation, a stepping mass ascends to create four local promontories of form. Note the ragged edges, back-side alignment of stepping to the lot line and expressive facade patterning.*

Figure 5 *Permutations. A consistent, limited palette of materials and orthogonal geometric manipulation create an extraordinary variety of local spaces, forms, and focal points. Decidedly sculptural and expressive, these coordinated systems of plane, mass, color, line, and space are almost a catalog of architectural potentials as explored in one small housing project.*

But the nearby country club provides an optional amenity for those who can afford it. Local bike and jogging paths lead to the nearby Tingly Lake and extend the confines of the site into a lovely landscape.

Beyond the positive site implications, the project itself presents a wide variety of unit types, from studio to four-bedroom. All have significant connection to the outdoors via patios and a series of exterior walks and steps. The four aforementioned four-bedroom penthouses have ascendant "skyplazas"—rooftop platforms from which to view the multiple vistas of pure landscape. These penthouses are often rented by four independent singles.

The accommodative number of unit types, totaling seventy-four units, affordable pricing of rentals, and beckoning community resources overcome the lack of project amenities. Some units have fireplaces, laundries, balconies, and enclosed garages. Top-level units have angled ceilings.

Interiors are functional, without the luster of expensive materials or detailing that might threaten the project's budget.

EFFICIENCY

Albuquerque has a relatively benign climate: A few light snows and a few 100-degree-plus days are rare extremes. Solar overheating is the only major environmental liability in the seldom overcast conditions. The Beach eschews much of the solar intrusion by turning a blank wall or two to the south and by using the folds of the project's mass for self-shading.

Low-cost individual heat-pump electric HVAC units were chosen for their low purchase and installation costs. The cost per Btuh is relatively high for heating, but the season is short.

6

Figure 6 *Upper entry. As seen from the door, an elevated path has a local focus (the centered square perforation set at eye level). The shade, painted-on patterning, and multiple wall stepping enliven a potentially prosaic space.*

Figure 7 *Interior. A top-floor living area with sequestered kitchen and transcendant clerestory glazing. Note corner fireplace, tiled entry (left center), and large-scale opening to a narrow gallery space beyond.*

8

Figure 8 *Bird's eye. A celebrational stepping of height and perimeter create an extraordinary form, in concert with its distant mountain focus (upper right) and in distinction to the fluid strip it addresses (lower left).*

Figure 9 *Section. Taken at the southern wide end of the project, the highest point of the design, a common parking entry access level forms the plinth upon which three levels of units are built (left). This four-story projection occurs only at the point where the three-bedroom duplex creates one of four minimountains. Across from this summit is a more typical three-story section.*

9

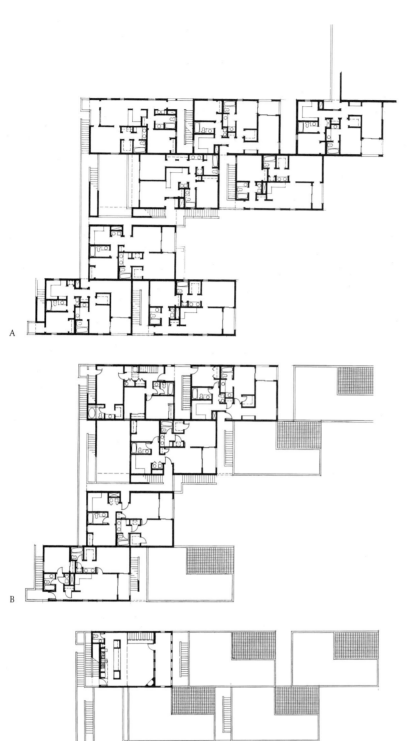

A

B

C

Figure 10 *Plans. Taken at the south end of the project.*

A (Lower) *although the form appears to turn corners, the units all share a single orientation. Set above the ground level, this plan has several variations on two-bedroom single-story-unit plans. Note the use of covered corner open terraces which address the mountain view and the multitude of open access stairs, walkways, and small outdoor spaces.*

B (Middle) *As the building mass ascends, edge units step back, and three of the eight units are not projected up to this level. Note that even on this elevated level, each unit is accessed directly from the outside.*

C (Top) *The solitary penthouse forms the only duplex of these related units and creates the minimountaintops which form formal foci in the context of the stepping mass. Note that this is the only unit to have a living area fireplace and that its public spaces are set above the lower level of three bedrooms and entry. There is also a private, although outdoor, back stair from master bedroom to kitchen.*

Photographs by Timothy Hursley

Intricately Financed
Nonprofit Development

YORKSHIRE TERRACE

Los Angeles

John V. Mutlow, *Architect*

OBJECTIVES

Yorkshire Terrace is one of a growing number of residential projects that use a dazzling array of financing techniques to produce housing for the working poor. In the wake of a 75 percent cutback in federal funding, nonprofit sponsors and their architects have learned to integrate several sources of financing to make such projects feasible. To the complexity of designing and building to meet the special needs of the working poor is added, in these cases, the inordinant complexities of applying for a variety of bureaucratically intricate sources of funding. In the case of Yorkshire Terrace, the task was further compounded by the challenge of building on a tough in-fill site.

John V. Mutlow had prepared for the task. He, like a few other architects nationally, has done considerable work with nonprofit housing sponsors. In fact, his first job after graduation was as the director of housing and planning for the Pico-Union Housing Corporation, the nonprofit organization that sponsored Yorkshire Terrace. With Pico-Union, Mutlow has done nine residential projects for limited-income households; Yorkshire Terrace is one of the more complex and ambitious, although smaller of the lot.

Low- and moderate-income families do not have sufficient funds to attract the private market to build new housing for them. In cities like Los Angeles there is insufficient decent existing housing to meet the need. Often, the cost of rehabilitating existing substandard housing is considerably in excess of building new. In this pithy arena, the typical profit-oriented builder does not regularly compete. It is an area of housing development that has attracted atypical developers—some private, many nonprofit. Many of the state and federal subsidy programs provide financial assistance only to, or primarily to, nonprofit organizations because the subsidy may not be given to benefit a profit-oriented developer.

Figure 1 *Site. Two unit blocks, an L and a wall, define two thresholds. These thresholds define the major longitudinal and minor crossaxial axes. The intersection of the primary-entry cross axis (right) and the central major axis is celebrated with a tiled pavilion, while intermediate cross-axial points are denoted with square tiled pads.*

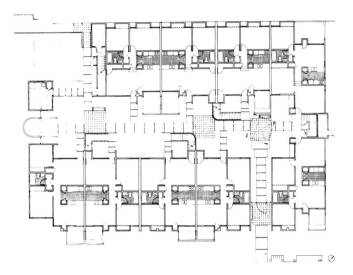

Figure 2 *Streetscape. A variegated, crenelated facade has its rhythm punctuated by a raised entry pavilion. Shade and light, color and mass, and material and form are interwoven to create a positive systematic image. Note the miniarcade of trees at entry, and slight berm of earth easing the long edge of construction.*

In recent years, these nonprofits have proved increasingly capable of putting together complicated financing packages and, as evident in Yorkshire Terrace, of aspiring to excellence in architecture. This flexibility has made the nonprofit developer very useful to cities as well. The City of Los Angeles had invested a considerable effort in the neighborhood, particularly in the rehabilitation of large old Victorian homes. Three such houses occupied the Pico-Union half acre, but were deemed structurally unsound and demolished, leaving an ugly gap in the neighborhood.

What cities aspire to in such community development initiatives is to reach a taking-off point at which reinvestment will occur naturally. In the early stages of these efforts, nonprofit, more than for-profit, developers are willing to take risks and begin development. The addition of eighteen well-designed, low-rise homes on this half-acre site was a move to reinvest in the neighborhood. To do it right, the density had to be modest, the design excellent, and the overall effect positive. A nonprofit sponsor rose to the challenge. The motivation can be traced to the fact that the nonprofit itself was created out of, and organized to serve, the neighborhood.

3

4

Figure 3 *Courtyard. A rich, progressive space, culminated from this vantage with the skewed pavilion (lower right). Human-scaled elements (walls, seating, planting) diffuse the potential for oppression by the two-story buildings which form this linear space.*

Figure 4 *Entry. A local center formed by symmetry and the isolated projection of the gabled roof. Plantings, openings, and color all conspire to reinforce the focal point. Note the preserved existing tree (right).*

Figure 5 *Applied elements. The secondary components of a diagrammatic plan (lowest) are "explicated" via graphic projection. The middle axonometric shows outside wall parts and courtyard stair and wall pieces. The top axonometric shows courtyard wall appliqués, with pavilions and paths further projected above this image.*

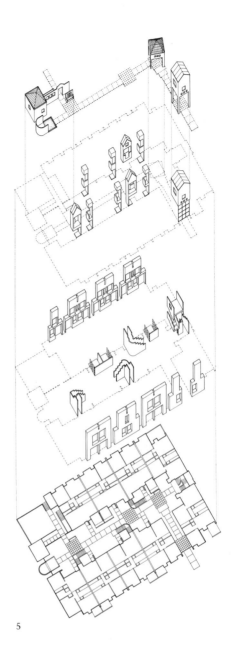

5

COMMUNITY AND ENVIRONMENT

This project, as distinct from most others, is of the community. The area is a Mexican-American neighborhood; Pico-Union Housing Corporation is affiliated with the local neighborhood council. Its central objective is to serve and enhance that neighborhood. It does this through affordability, moderate scale, sociability, quality design, and efficiency.

Yorkshire Terrace was built for less than $50 per square foot, or about $42,000 per unit—a remarkable accomplishment even in the mid-1980s. Mutlow's principal concession to affordability was the 800-square-foot size of the development's two-bedroom units. He compensated by the addition of an internal courtyard which serves all the units and tends to expand the sense of scale of the individual units. Its physical orientation greatly aids energy efficiency, which enhances both comfort and ongoing affordability.

Although the city's regulations allowed twenty-eight units on the site, Mutlow felt that a lower-density, two-story approach would be better for family housing, after reflecting on the spotted history of higher-rise subsidized housing for families. The architect worked hard to relieve even that lower density by the use of the internal courtyard and open parking areas—spaces that tend to mitigate the modest vertical volume of the buildings.

This moderated density is softened further by thoughtful massing articulation; the use of subtle color variations; attention to landscaping, including generous use of palm trees; and the integration of gabled elements throughout the development. The palm trees and landscaping on the perimeter and the choice of exterior materials and colors that reflect the hues of the larger neighborhood bespeak the project's sensitivity to the area from which it arose and which it serves.

ORGANIZATION

There are two clear organizing principles evidenced by this project. The first is the economic imperative. This design absolute keys the second large-scale organizational overlay—the ubiquitous application of orthogonal bearing-wall construction which responds to the simple rectangular site. These two predominant concerns foster a light application of secondary design features. A system of applied architectural elements play off of the simple project massing. Color is used subtly, yet effectively. The detailing of all these evocative features has a foundation in the surrounding community.

The large-scale site organization and construction techniques are quite simple. The short-leg end of the L outline block of units aligns with a second block of units, forming a row. These blocks are formed with two layers of one-story units. Between the two blocks is a processional court. Gaps between the blocks are made to be celebrational thresholds. All parts of the project are clad in stucco. Project corners are recessed. Parking is half-buried under half of the long side of the L block, raising its "back" side floor level three steps up. These broad-stroke moves are given life by the application of the subtext of large-scale architectural elements. Viewed as components by the architect, they may be described as off-the-rack parts which might be applied to any mute building mass. They include:

1. *Entry Pavilions.* The street entry is a gable-roofed pavilion suspended above a large-scale security gate, creating the highest massing element and a formal front door. The parking-side entry uses a detached laundry—a pyramidally roofed outbuilding—and extends a simple perforated wall with gable-topped entry opening. Both elements are lower than the predominant project massing, creating a quiet "back door."

2. *Facade Lamination.* A 30-inch layer of plan extension is occasionally added to the potentially flat long walls of the project. These projections form closets, window bays, and second-floor access landings. They provide an inexpensive means of distinguishing units and create surface variation with a consistent vocabulary of appliqués.

3. *Stairs.* Overtly "tack-on" parts, these elements are both highly animated—by color, stepping walls and curves—and are undeniably functional.

4. *Incidental Elements.* A pavilion with a pyramidal screen roof is set at the juncture of the courtyard's two main axes—it has a tilted orientation which indicates each axis is not a dead end as seen from the courtyard's entry thresholds. Benches are richly colored, aggrandized in shape, and integrated with the pavilion and transition points in the processional court to help create subspaces.

6a

6b

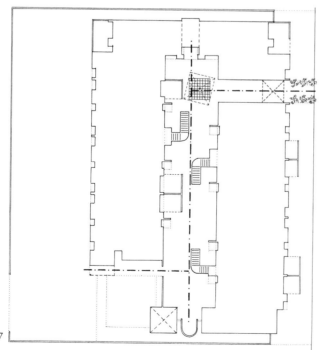

7

8

Figure 6 *Courtyard axes. A linear path is activated and received by applied elements. Tile pads connected by concrete sidewalks interact with projecting stair elements. These stairs utilize curves and large-scale stepping to celebrate their special status. The crucial pavilion (as focal point in a and framing vantage in b) violates the rectilinear organization of the units, tilting to recognize each axis. Note that a dark curved wall receives the axis projecting out from the pavilion.*

Figure 7 *Parti sketch. This diagram shows the three major axes (dark dash-dot lines), incidental pavilions with crossed dashed lines, and building perimeter. Note how projecting stairs create intermediate spaces along the major axis, while wall elements both receive axes and help define their edges.*

Figure 8 *Section. Cut across both blocks, through the courtyard and parking, cars can barely be seen at left, causing the left unit block to bump up, which creates higher ceilings addressing the courtyard and a level change at the middle of the plan. Note the projected cornices and parapets.*

Photographs by Marvin Rand

5. *Ground Surfacing.* Square gridded tile pads are set at transition spaces—at the pavilion, between two stairs, at entry conditions—and help to create local spaces in the context of a long courtyard space.

6. *Walls.* Each ground-level unit pushes out a one-story, freestanding wall element with flanking steel-mesh fences to create private outdoor space.

Those elements all sit below or rise above the block cornice lines, creating a lively sense of formal manipulation. Color is applied to each of these elements—sometimes subtly, sometimes boldly to reinforce their particular presence and identity. Windows vary in scale, form corners, and interweave with the simple openings found in the applied elements to create a consistent sense of skin. Plantings weave in and about all the activity for a natural counterpoint. All these elements form or interact with the two main processional axes. In short, stage-set architectural animation enlivens a potentially rude project.

The nuts-and-bolts organizing features of this project are similar to any number of similar low-budget designs. A structural system of simple span framing and bearing-wall support is enlivened by making an interplay of two bay dimensions. Units are consistently flipped, matching like functions between units. The architect then runs a layer of wet functions down the middle of the blocks and across the bearing-wall orientation, allowing living and bedroom spaces to have natural light. The L block orients bedrooms to the "outside" and the public spaces to the "inside," facing the courtyard. The street-addressing block takes a natural approach: Bedrooms are placed in the narrow bay, facing both courtyard and street, and the public spaces are in the wider bay, with similar dual orientation. All room sizes were rigidly compliant with the Housing and Urban Development's explicit regulations, forming a spatial determinant of absolute design impact.

Without the clarity of site organization, the playful appliqués would be so much pointless window dressing. But with the stark realities of budgetary control having absolute sway over geometry, material, and mass, the architect could not escape the rationality of the project's image; he merely recognized the need for psychic relief. He created the invigorating subtext of artful elements in concert with the dominant form and organization of his site plan. As such, the project accommodates both its ethical and aesthetic goals.

INTERIORS, AMENITIES, AND SERVICES

There is one overriding amenity in this project—affordability. The charming courtyard, private entries, and private outdoor space for ground-level units are all positive amenities not often encountered in projects such as this.

The materials used are functional. Spaces set at bare minimums (800-square-foot two-bedroom units). There is little storage space, no secondary functional space (family, den, or office), and one full bath per two-bedroom unit. Laundry is centralized, as is parking.

EFFICIENCY

The architects try to make up for the lack of air conditioning by the use of "cool" colors—in this case, green. Since this project is located in balmy Los Angeles, the cooling costs would be assumed to be the greatest environmentally determined financial concern. But since these concerns have been limited by budgetary constraints to a coat of paint, a great deal of the energy-efficiency imperative has been obviated.

Visionary Studies

There may truly be a glimpse of the twenty-first century in this section. Six visionary studies conclude the book. They are all yet to be built, perhaps in several cases because they are waiting patiently for the future to unfold.

One is an energy-efficient, "adaptive reuse" project in the inner city, the kind of project celebrated by a national commission, but too seldom executed. There are two design competition projects that would fit perfectly into the urban fabric but are waiting for the right land-use agencies and financing sources. There are designs for the redevelopment of two large existing structures that serve new markets but present special strategic problems in turning the corner from old use to new.

Finally, there is Daniel Solomon's offering: the Vest Pocket Community in Fairfax, California. There will be much continuity of design and development in the housing field over the next two decades, but there must be new responses to the challenge of housing smaller, more diverse households, utilizing remnant parcels, and conserving the environment through better use of developed areas. Solomon's project does all three. What is remarkable is that this project seems to combine the influences of a number of recent projects into a truly new form of housing.

The forces of continuity do not need a book like this. Where existing forms, financing, and needs are at play, existing solutions will work as long as the demand for them is strong. This book focuses on innovation, on the changes architects and houses have had to make to respond to the "new" in America and the undeniable needs of today and tomorrow. By ending with visionary studies, and particularly with the Vest Pocket Community, this point is meant to stay with the reader, along with the knowledge that our architects and the attached form of housing are moving ahead as quickly as the events which mold them.

A Toehold on the Urban Turf for the Homeless

SNOWDON PROJECT

Syracuse, New York

Syracuse University School of Architecture

Professor Grace Coleman/Peter Arsenault, *Architect*

OBJECTIVES

One of the great contemporary challenges is the explosive growth of homeless and near-homeless families and individuals. In almost any metropolitan newspaper, one can read harrowing stories of homeless children living in faraway motels and commuting back to their former schools, of homeless men shoehorned into temporary shelters, or of near-frozen family members gathered over a grate on a winter's evening.

The numbers are truly staggering and the tragedy enormous. Estimates of homeless people in the United States range up to 4 million individuals. Informed predictions are that this number could grow fivefold in the next fifteen years. The lion's share of these people are children and their mothers. Of the remainder, only a small fraction are ex-criminals, deadbeat single men, drifters, and alcoholics—the various stereotypes that many hold of the homeless.

This is, at root, a problem of housing and economics. In many areas the housing stock that has traditionally served the poor is disappearing. This is due to demolition, condemnation, and competition. The competition comes from two sources. The first is the return to some urban areas of young, upwardly mobile individuals and couples, charmed by urban life and hardy enough to cope with the challenge of transitional neighborhoods. As mentioned earlier, this has been called ''gentrification.'' The second is from the near-homeless, the working poor, and moderate-income families, who themselves feel the housing-cost squeeze and now compete for homes in neighborhoods where gentrification is the remotest possibility. Working families who live in public housing cannot leave, as it was thought they would, when their incomes rose, because there is nowhere to go. As a result, vacancy rates in public housing have shrunk from 15 percent in the mid-1960s to

Figure 1 *Site. The only triangular building in its context, the Snowdon sits at the junction of five street corners where its presence is ignored, and perhaps irrevocably compromised, by the elevated superhighways which cut through the neighborhood.*

Figure 2 *Existing building. The building's corner posture, relatively grand scale and heavily articulated facade make this structure a local landmark—a status which is reinforced by its history.* (Photograph by Michelle Frankfurter, Syracuse Newspapers)

1

2

3 percent today. In short, if you are poor, or near-poor, in many areas, there is nowhere to live.

It is a problem of economics for several reasons. First, the cost of constructing new housing or of rehabilitating existing housing to create more places to live has far outstripped the ability of low- and moderate-income families to afford, even with a reasonable government subsidy. Second, federal subsidies for low-income housing have dropped from over $35 billion in 1980 to $7 billion in 1988. Third, our employment patterns are shifting, so that there are few jobs in most areas for those homeless and near-homeless individuals who are trained to work, which heightens the need for some form of subsidy.

Against this tide, there is some hope. A few states are appropriating helpful sums of money to partly replace federal largess. An impressive crop of nonprofit developers has emerged with great creativity to develop housing for lower-income families. See, for example, our description in the previous section of Yorkshire Terrace in Los Angeles. More recently, the American Institute of Architects has entered the fray through its Search for Shelter Project.

It was Search for Shelter, lead by Peter Arsenault, a local architect, that tackled the Snowdon building in Syracuse. This stately masonry structure was built in 1902 to provide 36 luxury apartments for the area's well-to-do. Over the years, it has been reconfigured into 165 small apartments, mostly single-room-occupancy quarters, housing the homeless. The area is "gentrifying," the building is for sale, and the eviction notices ready to be printed, unless Search for Shelter is successful in funding its recent design for the improvement of the building.

The architect-led effort has already accomplished a great deal. The owner is willing to negotiate a sale. The neighborhood has gotten involved and has supported the continuation of occupancy by lower-income individuals of the Snowdon building. A broad coalition has met on many occasions to study the building, to determine the housing and social needs of its occupants, and to consider architectural designs for the building's redevelopment. This coalition has identified New York State's innovative Homeless Housing Assistance Program as the likely source of funding. Should this momentum continue, the initiative could work. If it does, it will be a proud progeny of the Search for Shelter pilot project, which led to the renovation of a dilapidated hotel in Shreveport, Louisiana, for occupancy by the homeless.

COMMUNITY AND ENVIRONMENT

The impact of the proposed Snowdon redevelopment plan on the community is seen very differently from the other projects covered in this book. What is at issue here is a matter of social justice as measured by the ability of a community to retain diversity and fairness in its demography. The law of planning and zoning, the federal and most state constitutions, and a broad body of housing statutes all call for local governments to act to maintain a broad demographic base, which includes the provision of decent housing for the poor.

The challenge of Snowdon, of the Shreveport hotel, and of the many similar initiatives unfolding throughout the country is to find ways of providing permanent places for the poor to live in communities of all kinds, so that those communities can be economically integrated, as they have traditionally been.

The efforts of the Syracuse coalition, aided by the Syracuse University School of Architecture and assisted by architect Peter J. Arsenault, are focused on transforming the building itself into a supportive community for homeless families and individuals, many of whom need a special place to live. The proposed design, one submitted by Alejandro Ceppi, a fourth-year Syracuse architectural student seeks to convert the small apartments into better-designed living quarters and to enhance these small spaces with a central dining and social area, a welcoming entrance space, a mechanical wheelchair lift, and room for the provision of social services.

As of this writing, Catholic Charities, the Northeast Hawley Development Association (the neighborhood group), the local American Institute of Architects chapter, the university, and a group of cooperating businesses are pursuing acquisition and funding in a spirited effort to provide one more desperately needed model of how this most serious of our country's social problems can be solved.

ORGANIZATION

Essentially this building is organized by its existing V-shaped footprint. Two wings join at a hub, creating a space between them and a focused entry at their juncture. The condition of the existing floor joist necessitated a structural reorganization. It would have been easy to simply stiffen, augment, and selectively replace those inadequate members which have caused the floors of this building to sag seriously. But in conceptual projects, risks can be taken to inspire the realization of the concept.

In light of this inspired musing, the program mentioned above created a "separation imperative." Where transient and often chaotic lifestyles are embraced by housing, sound separation and structural security between units can often enable disparate neighbors to bypass each other. Rather than keep the framing in its present orientation (perpendicular to the long walls of the wings), the designers reoriented both the framing and the bearing conditions. The long spans of the existing framing were broken up by intermediate wood-frame walls of the interior corridor. But in a bold stroke the designers opted to create a new parallel bearing-wall system *within* the wings, set perpendicularly to the exterior walls, thereby reorienting the basic floor framing direction to span between these new walls at 90° to the original span.

These new bearing walls separate the new units. By this one move, sound separations are enhanced and the new masonry walls are durable enough to resist the onslaught of a rapidly changing use group. There is a tertiary benefit to this construction as well. It can be paced to allow existing tenants to remain as long as possible.

The second major move to recreate the existing building was also generated by the V-shaped building configuration. Originally a luxury apartment building with 36 units, this building has evolved to a single-room-occupancy building with 165 units. As such, it had no social spaces, creating the insensitive cubbyhole accommodations that simply prolong the nightmare of the homeless, accomplishing little to get the residents out of the institutional revolving door. The designers have seen the need to add service to safety and have proposed to construct new space in the first floor of the V to accommodate four social agencies. When combined with available basement space and some floor-level changes, this area becomes a "heart" of skylit space in a once heartless building. The building's entry would be accessible to the handicapped and visually controllable under this proposal.

To design for a higher goal than the common denominator of human storage can make a difference in long- and short-term accommodation of the desperate. In the process, a landmark building can be preserved, present residents respected, and some nice interior spaces created. Getting more than you hoped for is not a mindset typically associated with the homeless. But dark clouds can have silver linings, and it is hoped that the silver in this case extends to funding some sensitive and visionary work of altruistic origins.

INTERIORS, AMENITIES, AND SERVICES

The interiors of these units would be of the spartan, high-durability kind, designed for low maintenance and longevity. All windows would be replaced, all interior surfaces new. Sound-deafening factors and the durability of partitions have been discussed, as has the first-floor space devoted to social service agencies. But the greatest amenity this project offers is hope. By the creation of ninty-six single-room-occupancy units, thirty-six efficiencies, and twenty-four one- and two-bedroom apartments, a variety of homeless households are accommodated.

How can you measure the relief from stress that a clean, safe, and commodious space gives? The sad truth is that for the homeless, "amenity" means "survival." The brighter hope is that good design and supportive services can create greater independence and a transition to a fuller life for the homeless in such urban places.

EFFICIENCY

The project calls for the thorough gutting of the existing building's structural and mechanical infrastructure. It is presumed that the materials and equipment used will maximize the efficiency of winter heating in the cold climate Syracuse offers. With so many small separate units with sporadic occupancy, the localization of all thermostat controls makes a great deal of sense.

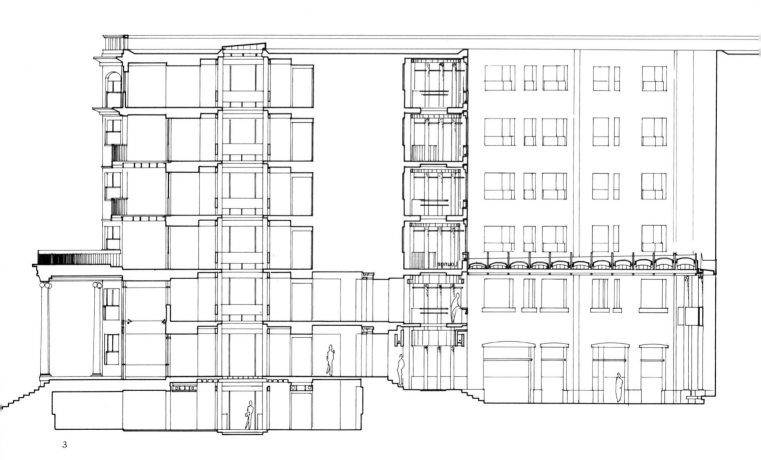

3

4

Figure 3 *Section. Cut at the crotch, through the main entry and new lobby, the continuities of lobby light well ascending through all levels (left), and stacked rotunda lounges (center) are flanked by existing entry (far left) and new public space (right). Note how the existing inner facade extends into the new double-height public space and how the bottom level of this facade is opened up, creating piers. The glazed roof of the public space would also allow those within it to appreciate the view of the exposed facades ascending above roof level. The public service agency spaces are set below-grade (left), with natural light gained through a glass-block floor oriented to the through-building light well. Note how a new double-height space is created at the entry, and outdoor overlooks orient out over the existing entry portico (left).*

Figure 4 *Common space. The new construction is set between the two existing wings of the building's V. This space serves as the living room for the entire structure. Its level is set at a grade 6 feet below the existing first floor of the building. A glazed roof is indicated, as is a curvilinear crotch at the juncture of the existing wings. These details are costly, but hopefully inspirational when presented on paper. Note the single-loaded, half-floating second-floor corridor (upper right), which has its view of the space filtered by the clerestory level openings of the existing wall, now bared. The supporting piers are removed for visual clarity and reveal the freestanding walls—including information and storage pieces—used here to obscure the unit entrances.*

Figure 5 *Structural axonometrics.
The existing building* (a) *is shown to be
a simple three-bay bearing-wall system,
where the central-frame corridor walls
proved inadequate and created a great
deal of sagging. The proposed renovation*
(b) *is a completely new system,
designed to bypass the existing masonry
perimeter walls and create all-new
bearing walls, which would be set at
right angles to the exterior walls.
Although costly, this proposal allows
for maximal sound separation. This
proposal also gives the opportunity to
do the work on a piecemeal basis,
ensuring a minimal amount of eviction
during construction. Note that the new
system respects all existing openings in
the exterior facades and that it is to
have a concrete floor decking, providing
a horizontal layer of sound deadening.*

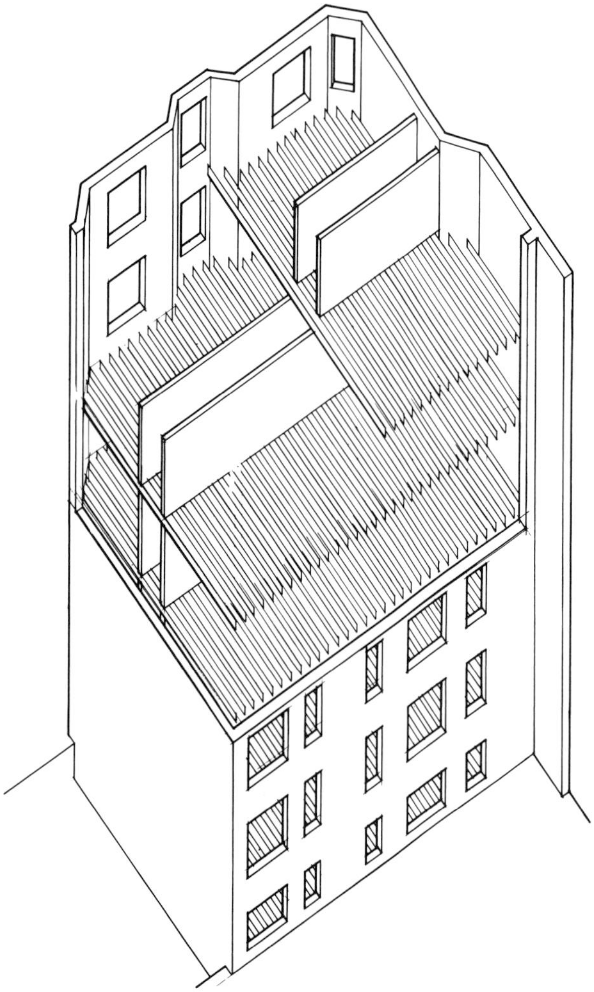

5a

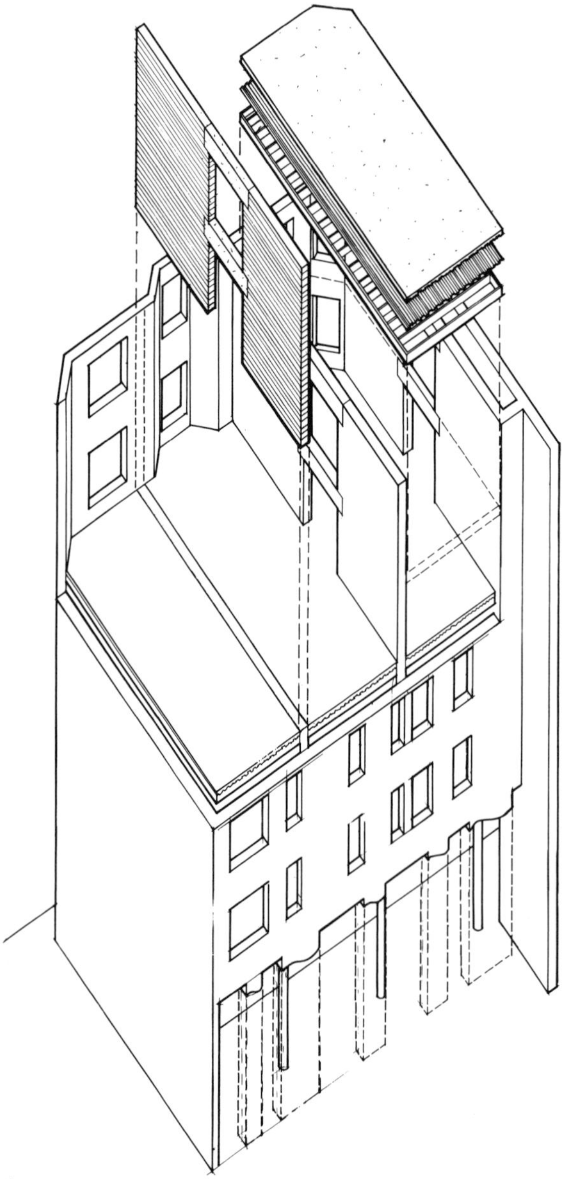

5b

Figure 6 *Existing plan diagram. Shown at the entry level (without room partitions), the building has three major circulation cores and two centralized bath cores. The double-loaded central corridors connect the three stair wells. Note the indication of the existing simple-span framing (the dash-dot lines). Note, also, the bays, bevels, and bows which highlight and subdivide the V plan perimeter.*

Figure 7 *Entry level. The prow of the form, always the building's main access point, has the existing circulation core relocated further back into the building's "crotch," creating a legitimate lobby space, flanked by building administration offices and lounges. The wing circulation cores are kept back in the same relative slots, but pushed out to the street side. Crucial to the entire scheme is the creation of the in-fill public area at the space between the wings. Accessed by a little rotundaesque space (mimicking the entry porch), this space has a glazed roof, making a hospitable living room for the entire building. Note that the existing inner-wing walls have been bared and left freestanding and that they have been relegated to a pier support function for the floors above. Note how all the level changes (including entry) have wheelchair lifts.*

Figure 8 *Typical upper floor. New plan elements are carried up from the entry level: the "lobby" (with a central opening on all levels to the ground-floor lobby), the "rotunda" lounges, and the circulation cores. The apartments (with their own living and bath spaces) are located at the wing ends and crotch. Single-occupancy rooms stretch between these end points and have common baths at the crotch and wing ends. This floor shows how the newly inserted short-direction masonry bearing walls would form each living space and how they would mesh with the building's existing window and facade patterns. Note how the new transverse bearing walls are laminated with storage cubbies and how entries have minor walls and closets located about them to create a more private access.*

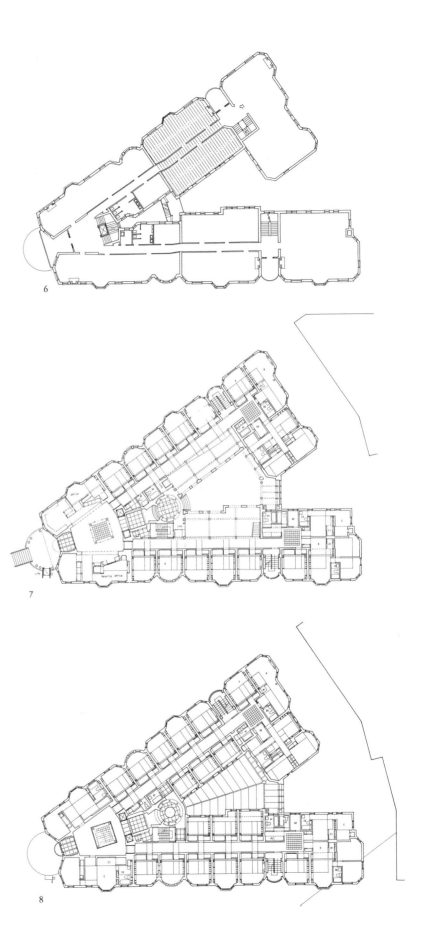

6

7

8

Adaptive Reuse—
In Response to a National Priority

---

424 WEST 33rd STREET

New York, New York

Banwell, White & Hemberger, *Architects*

OBJECTIVES

In the early eighties, the National Council on Development Choices for the 1980s, appointed by the President, studied a number of national development trends which it found disturbing and then issued a report with recommendations for the future. Its report was highly praised and endorsed by many prestigious national organizations including the U.S. Conference of Mayors and the National Governors Association.

A number of the key recommendations of the council underline the importance of the plans of Banwell, White & Hemberger for the solid old building at 424 West 33rd Street in Manhattan. Their plans envisioned the conversion of this 75-year-old factory building to a 1980s residential loft condominium complex. Their primary objective was to renew an unused building, retaining its best qualities (extraordinary structural strength, sound resistance, and location) while increasing its size and completely reworking its interiors, mechanical systems, and glazing to accommodate the new use imposed and to maximize energy efficiency.

The building, located on the west side in Manhattan's midtown area, is situated close to mass transit; water and sewer systems; and public, commercial, recreational, and cultural services. It is a ready, extant resource desiring little material input to capably serve succeeding generations. In the trade, this redevelopment proposal is called "adaptive reuse," which stands for the retrofitting of an old, underutilized structure for a new use, more adapted to the present.

The council's recommendations unequivocally endorse such efforts:

1. It warns that "the development and redevelopment of communities must be based, in large degree, on practices to conserve energy. Buildings themselves must

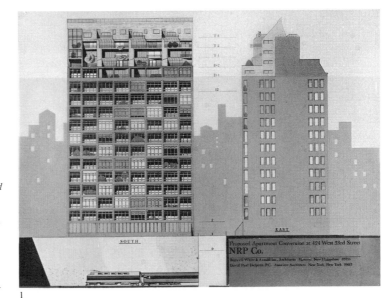

Figure 1 *Proposed—south and east. The structural grid is exposed and added upon. A progressive articulation addressing the sun, all new elements respect the given plinth of construction.*

Figure 2 *Existing site—south. An archetypal example of loft building. Windows respect the structural grid. Note the sheer retaining wall at bottom.*

1

be made more energy efficient, and land use patterns must provide better opportunities to save on transportation energy."

2. It suggests that "revitalization is a way to upgrade portions of built-up areas, salvaging what is still usable and taking advantage of extant facilities. The Council defines revitalization to include the adaptive reuse of structures for purposes different from their original ones."

3. It adds that "existing buildings are another resource that should not be wasted. Much precious development capital can be saved by rehabilitating or adapting buildings to new uses."

COMMUNITY

The project's neighborhood is a mix of large civic structures such as Penn Station, Madison Square Garden, and the General Post Office, other similar underutilized factory buildings, office towers, retail shops, and growing number of residential buildings. The structure itself had long since ceased to be a factory and was partially vacant, costing the owner dearly in lost revenue. This is the type of situation that New York City's tax abatement programs were designed to correct, by encouraging rehabilitation with a promise of lowered taxes.

Despite all these public pronouncements and programs, community reaction to the proposed retrofit and expansion was not positive. The architects and owner advocated a five-story addition to be built on top of the existing twelve-story structure and the complete reconstruction of the interior and exterior. This type of change can be threatening. In some cases, neighbors fear losing their homes through gentrification. In others, the prospect of added density raises fears of more traffic, people, and deliveries that test the capacities of neighbors to cope. In the face of citizen opposition, the developer's request for a variance to change the use of the building was denied, and the proposal is in limbo.

The Council on Development Choices warns also about resistance to positive change: "Citizen groups may resist many of the changes that would benefit consumers and communities for various reasons." The council heard much testimony about the type of information campaigns and mature public decision making that are necessary to shape and overcome public opinion. Perhaps, in time, this visionary proposal will reemerge, maybe even with the support of the neighbors.

Figure 3 *Section. The new construction steps back from the perimeter of the existing building, allowing most spaces to directly experience the outdoors and be bathed in sunlight. This form conjures up the imagery of a jewel set in the context of a prosaic plinth.*

4

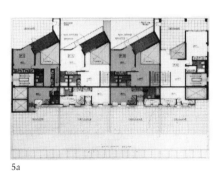

5a

5b

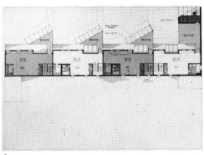

5c

Figure 4 *Model. The vertical components of the proposed new penthouse construction are oriented to the regulating lines of the existing construction below, while its facade angles to meet the morning sun.*

Figure 5 *Plans. a,b,c. Three of five levels are shown, each having terrace and sun space, most face toward the southeasterly sunlight.*

ENVIRONMENT

This project exists in an urban context, but this particular site has several distinct benefits. First, its structure, designed for the heavy loading of a factory, required no augmentation, even for the addition of five more floors. Secondly, the steel-frame style of construction allowed for extreme plan and facade flexibility. The building was also extraordinarily deep (90 feet), allowing for an efficient use of the plan area and the existing vertical circulation core locations. Lastly, the particular block that this building was situated upon had its back-side facing due south over a wide expanse of railroad tracks, recessed several stories below-grade. This assured that nothing would be built on either long side of the building, allowing for a high degree of interior amenity and passive solar applicability. Views are excellent in almost all directions, catching the Empire State Building to the east and the Hudson River to the west. The existing exterior of the building is very straightforward with some ornamental cave brackets on the north facade.

ORGANIZATION

The existing orthogonal structural cage is the dominant organizing influence on the final project's design. With the typical urban zero-setback lot coverage, there is little room for formal expression, save the proposed penthouse addition to the building's roof.

Despite the radical limitations of urban construction (extraordinary costs, heavy code restrictions, integration with existing infrastructure), it is the desire for passive solar retrofit that dominates nearly every design step taken in this project. There are three areas where solar-sensitive design has had a marked impact on the buildings' organization:

1. *Skin.*   The exterior building was to be reglazed with new windows, and the total glass area was to be increased to the south and diminished to the north.

2. *Interior.*   Southerly glazing is set before sun spaces, which in turn are set before trombe walls—designed to absorb winter solar heat and block summer sun. A layer of applied insulation is added to all exterior walls.

3. *Top.*   The form, orientation, and glazing of the five-story fourteen-unit penthouse addition is determined to maximize both solar penetration and passive summer airflow. This addition is meshed with the main building mass by recessing its form into the top floor.

The resulting units, created by the interface between existing structure and applied solar-determined retrofit, range in size from studios (700 square feet) to two bedrooms (1400 square feet). They would have had commodious spaces with 40 percent of the units having two exterior walls.

Clearly, this scheme addresses the reuse of a standardized structural system in compliance with specific zoning laws to create a thoroughly transformed building. Its full embrace of view, amenity, and space presents a standard for similar loft building conversions.

INTERIORS, AMENITIES, AND SERVICES

The reuse of the given grid in the rehabilitation of the factory building has not compromised the interiors of this project. In fact, the proposed penthouse addition created double-height spaces and greenhouses. In an unbuilt project, it is difficult to predict the finishes to be employed. But it is clear that the new glazing, sun spaces, and new public spaces created on the south side of the first floor of the project have tangibly benefited from the overlay of an energy consciousness upon its design.

EFFICIENCY

This project is a model of efficiency, from the reuse of the existing structure to the fundamental commitment to energy conservation and the use of the southern sun.

Of all the projects presented in this book, there is none that better presents a potentially prophetic design. There are thousands of buildings quite similar to 424 West 33rd Street all over America's urban centers. Studies done on this project presented at the Brookhaven National Laboratory show that this project saves up to 86 percent in heating costs over those for an average building of this type.

This same study was used to analyze all the systems employed and to reject many other options. The conclusions indicated that this proposed conversion made all the right moves. Beyond the capture of southerly winter light and the enhanced passive summer cooling of shading and ventilation, this project was to employ high-tech energy-conserving heating and cooling plants.

The open southerly view, deeper building section, and structural system suggested a passive solar solution, and the architects utilized all these advantages to create a model for thought. Thought born of our recent past might become a rapidly approaching future.

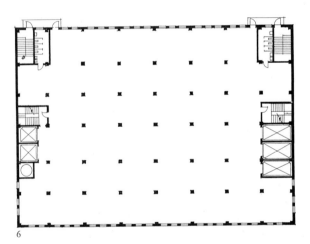

6

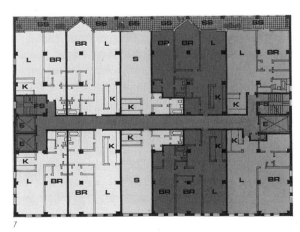

Figure 6 *Existing plan. A simple grid of columns, contained in a perimeter of glazing and masonry. Vertical cores of elevators, stair, and bathrooms are laminated to the east and west walls.*

Figure 7 *Proposed plan. Serving spaces (corridor, baths, storage, kitchen, utility) gravitate to the middle third of the plan along the logitudinal axis. The served spaces, bedroom and living, belly up to the building edge. The four corner units have a double-sided exposure.*

Photographs Courtesy of the Architect

7

Private Residences above Public Space

TOWN CENTER/HOME PARK

Fairfield, Connecticut

The Kagan Company, *Architects*

OBJECTIVES

Working on behalf of the town government, architects in the Kagan Company designed a sensitive residential project, around a quiet court and on top of a two-level parking structure that would be built as part of the project. The design is responsive to the need in downtown Fairfield, Connecticut, to balance commercial and office development with residential uses. The generic parking lot on which the development is projected to stand is an underutilized part of the urban fabric. The commercial area is in need of 24-hour-a-day residents to shop, work in offices, and breathe life into its daily pattern.

"Home Park," as a name, is full of import for America's developing areas. Fairfield County boasts some of the northeast's most pristine undeveloped areas, which are now subject to great development pressures. If this project is built in downtown Fairfield, those pressures will be reduced proportionately. The area is in need of reinforcement and balance. Laced into this development concept is parking for shoppers and residents, a quality residential community, shoppers for retail merchants, workers for nearby offices, new use for an underutilized parking area, more taxes for the town, better utilization of already built water and sewer systems, new users for the local library, and so on.

Despite all its advantages, this well-designed concept remains a paper plan for a better future. This is so largely because it stands outside the mainstream of the way in which development usually gets under way. To be built, Home Park must be supported by a creative, intricately financed public-private partnership, of the type that is much touted by recent federal administrations in Washington. The purchasers of the 40 residential units cannot pay to have the parking building built,

1

Figure 1 *Perspective. A rooftop garden community sits above a plinth of parking. The corners and center are eroded and celebrated to provide vertical access and visual focus. The prosaic parking function is ennobled by an architectural appliqué of large-scale well-trimmed openings, pilasters, and banding. Pyramidal roofs further obscure the nature of the housing's foundation.*

Figure 2 *Plans. Beveling corners help define a C-shaped form above the prototypical parking garage plan; this unsited model utilizes a two-ended ramp access. Typical unit plans can be seen within the context of these unit layouts. Note that the courtyard has its core perforated to create light wells and access. Corners are similarly exploited. A layering of unit types allows an equal number of grade-accessed units and individually accessed piggybacked duplexes.*

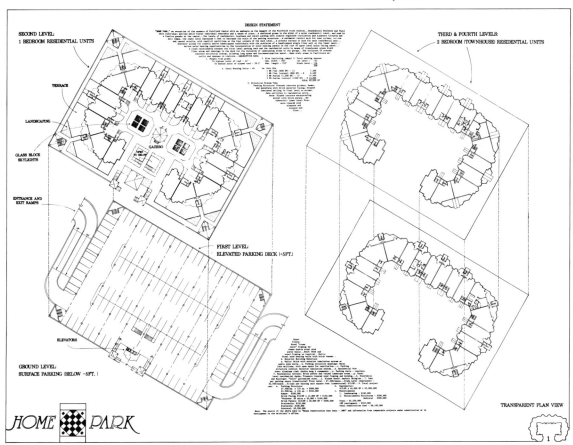

2

which is to contain 268 spaces and which will mostly benefit surrounding commercial and retail users.

This portion of the construction must be supported by the local tax base or through a special assessment district or through charges to users—arrangements which are all difficult to execute and which usually meet with the resistance of local taxpayers. State and federal infrastructure funds are dedicated these days to more serious needs, among them the repair of failing roadways and collapsing bridges, and the construction of critically needed infrastructure in newly developing areas. In this sense, Home Park is part of the prologue to the next chapter in public land planning and finance that needs soon to be written in this country.

The project confronts difficulties on the microlevel as well. How can one design a private residential community on top of a public space? How can one build a new parking and residential presence in the middle of a downtown area that is currently undergoing historic revitalization? The answers abound in the design presented by the Kagan Company.

The entire project maintains a reasonable profile, with a median point in the sloped-roof line of under 40 feet. Its design motif is taken from the historic Fairfield Train Station, and it uses design details that reinforce the historic character of the area in general.

The residential project, itself, is considerably buffered from the public spaces below. It is constructed on a quiet court "deck" over the second level of parking. On that deck is landscaping—trees, hedges, and lawns—and a central gazebo, inviting pedestrian pathways leading to pavilions on the perimeter. The forty homes are to be owned separately by their occupants and are made personal by separate entrances, private decks and terraces, and careful unit design.

COMMUNITY AND ENVIRONMENT

As much as any project in this publication, Home Park is devoted to serving both the community and the environment. This is so for all the reasons presented above. It is a beacon of balanced development, so desperately needed to enhance built areas and to reduce development pressures on the suburban fringe. The careful work of the architects in enhancing the historic character of the downtown only reinforces this point. For the same reasons, Home Park would attempt to do much in the area of environmental conservation.

The project works in many ways. It is a public service. Its costs are reasonable. It serves the environment. The architectural work is excellent. The building industry knows how to build it. Home buyers would accept it. But, it waits for the development of another technology, one centered in political science and public finance that will make such visionary ideas possible.

ORGANIZATION

An idealized design solution has abstract organizing features. Here, without a specific site (except for the general locale of a coastal Connecticut town), this project utilizes three simple organizational criteria.

First, the given contextual aesthetics of the town mandate the exterior detailing of this project. Gables, hipped roofs, bay windows, heavy trim, and Palladian allusions are all found in downtown Fairfield.

Second, and related to the first criterion, the zoning laws of Fairfield must be considered. Overall heights and setbacks are set in the local building code.

Last, and most importantly, this scheme utilizes a 268-space two-level parking garage. The garage acts as a structural, formal and functional plinth for the residential component. Its perimeter fits a typical small-town site. Its access points are, by definition, idealized.

In this tandem scheme, it is the access and circulation of the residents which could be problematic at best. It is tough enough to create a sense of ownership within a standard multiunit site, but to enter your unit via a parking garage set above street level is an extraordinarily difficult design problem.

To relieve the potential for a rude access, the architects recessed the garage's first-level 5 feet below-grade. The architects' second step was crucial, and transformed the entire project. Instead of thinking of the garage as a monolithic, immutable layer of structure, the garage itself is treated as a piece of architecture. The primary residential access point is created by an erosion of the center of one long edge of the garage. This void is partially filled in by three pavilions, all harboring circulation. Two flanking stair towers are situated at the corners of the entry recess and contain open-railed stairs. At the center of the recess is an enclosed elevator core. All three elements are at the scale of a typical town building and are detailed to reinforce the sense of scale.

This architectural encrypting of a prosaic structure is carried through to the facades of the garage itself. All four corners have expressive, stair tower pavilions which are completely open to the street. The wall-faced facades have half-rounded openings, heavily trimmed. The entire exterior is banded, pilastered, and corniced—in short, treated with aesthetic dignity. Once the visitor leaves the elevator core, he or she faces a courtyard defined by a C of three-story units, all contiguous. The front-entry perforation is carried into this level by several punctures of the plateau itself. First a bridge on axis with the elevator tower spans a hedge-lined, tree-filled void and is itself centered on an octagonal gazebo. Flanking the gazebo are two large-scale glass block skylights to the parking area below. Small lawns, entry stoops, trees, and gardens abound.

Beyond entry and circulation, the project carries out its horizontal layering up through the residential summit. The parking garage has a standard concrete structural frame, while the residential component utilizes parallel bearing walls set in line with the parking garage structure below. The first layer of housing is formed by twenty one-bedroom "flats," all accessed from the elevated court described earlier. Above these units are twenty two-bedroom duplexes, with code-compliant firestairs outside the courtyard, all with primary access points within the courtyard space.

Essentially what could be a significant design liability, the garage, creates instead a significant amenity. The elevation of the project presents logistical problems, but these problems are solved. The crucial difference that this design manifests is facilitated by its density. The units are small enough (as small as 600 square feet) to facilitate the tight C of construction. The architects utilized space-saving diagonal bearing walls at the block corners. The tightness creates an esplanade at the perimeter of the residential level, which is a viable buffer between the hubbub of the street and the quiet private life of a town resident. Secondarily, the inner court of this project is activated by the urban scale of its many entries, small-scale stoops, and rich architectural development. Its inward focus creates a quiet, civilized secondary world: secure, quiet, and peaceful.

INTERIORS, AMENITIES, AND SERVICES

In such a "paper" project, there are more questions than assured features. But it is clear that the architects have utilized a variety of design elements to accommodate both residential and commercial needs. As mentioned, trees are brought to the summit. Additionally, the unit-entry courtyard is a significant amenity, especially in the context of comparable village residences.

The living quarters are small, 600 to 800 square feet for a one-bedroom and 1200 to 1500 square feet for a two-bedroom unit. These are units for the young professional couple, for the single occupant, or perhaps for the empty nesters. The program does not call for social spaces or other services.

The interior amenities are sketchy, but bays, bows, and walkout terraces are employed. A triple layer of sound-deadening horizontal construction would be employed between parking and residential levels. Units would have laundries, but relatively small baths and kitchens.

Perhaps the greatest amenity such a scheme provides is its location. Without the subsidization of the parking garage, code-compliant non-high-rise construction might not be economically viable in town centers such as this.

EFFICIENCY

Given the level of detail and the absence of a specific site, it is difficult to know what steps would be employed to enhance efficiency beyond the inherent economies of multiunit construction.

LONGITUDINAL ELEVATION

Figure 3 *A proud, symmetrical front facade (above) has a crown of residential ambience which includes the use of shade trees. Central and flanking stair towers enhance the sense of architectural articulation. The side view (opposite, top) has a similar dignity, with the applied access ramp at its base. The sections (opposite, center and bottom) shows the two levels of parking and the interstitial insulation against both cold and noise. Note the tree wells, and the half-buried level of the first floor of parking. Note also that the 35-foot height restriction is adhered to and that the perimeter garage cornice effectively shields the project's true height.*

Drawings Courtesy of the Architect

SIDE ELEVATION

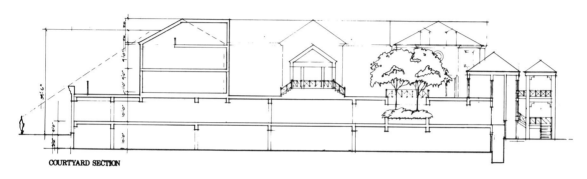

COURTYARD SECTION

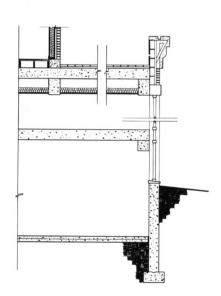

TYPICAL PERIMETER WALL SECTION   SCALE:1/2"-1'-0"

Sheltering Workers
for over a Century

THE RIVERSIDE BUILDINGS

Brooklyn, New York

Kliment & Halsbad Architects

OBJECTIVES

The historical legacy of these six-story masonry buildings in Brooklyn is considerable. They were built at the end of the nineteenth century as an inspired retort to the horrible tenement conditions in which workers at that time lived. A wealthy social reformer by the name of Alfred T. White became one of the earliest and, to this day, most successful housing activists in the country—a proud tradition in New York City. White joined a group of investors and constructed three significant projects for the working class, using and greatly improving on a model borrowed from London.

The tenements of the day had spawned terrible living conditions, which led to infant mortality rates exceeding 30 percent and to a host of other social ills. To create a more healthful environment, White constructed 280 small apartments at a depth of 40 feet with exterior staircases to provide light and air for each unit and to cut down on the spread of communicable disease. The units ranged in size from 350 to 540 square feet. This was accomplished by placing bathrooms in the basements and utilizing an all-purpose living room that included cooking facilities. The buildings were arranged on an acre-and-a-half site around a large internal courtyard which occupied over half the parcel and provided a considerable amenity in this rapidly urbanizing section of Brooklyn.

These developments were a dramatic success in their time. White's improvements on the design of "Improved Dwellings for the Laboring Classes," as the English model he emulated was called, were in turn adopted in London. He was instrumental in the thinking of the National Housing Association of the day, his design was used in other American cities, and, on his death, he was eulogized by President Taft as one who "led this country in improving the housing for the poor."

Figure 1 *Site. An L-shaped block addresses the existing street grid, while a new elevated highway swoops across the back. These two dominant site features define the courtyard.*

Figure 2 a *and* b. *Existing conditions. The street facade* (a) *evidences the rich detailing, surface manipulation, and material interaction which make this existing building a rare architectural gem. The courtyard* (b) *is an equally rare urban amenity; a city park, privately held and appreciated.*

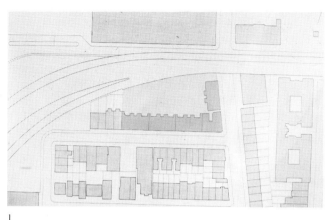

1

2

157

Since the project's completion in 1890, its environs have undergone much change. Most notably, just after World War II, the western half of the complex was demolished to make way for the Brooklyn-Queens Expressway. Since that time the buildings have steadily declined and are in a seriously deteriorated condition today.

Under the guidance of architects R. M. Kliment and Frances Halsbad, the brick-and-masonry buildings on the remaining 1 acre of the original site are poised for restoration and redevelopment. Phase one of this effort involved the recent refurbishing of the exteriors, including the replacement of windows, rebuilding and pointing of the masonry, the installation of a new roof and boiler plant, and the replacement in kind of all cast-iron columns at the balconies. In time, as units are vacated, the 156 remaining apartments will be reshaped into 100 larger flats, duplexes, and triplexes, ranging in size from 700 to 1600 square feet.

Again, investors are attracted to the buildings, this time because they would be involved in the restoration of buildings which have been designated landmarks on the National Register and which are included in the Brooklyn Heights Historic District. Using one of the few real estate tax incentives left in the Internal Revenue Code by the Tax Reform Act of 1986, investors will qualify for a 15 percent tax credit for the cost of restoration work that is done in conformance with the rigorous standards of the U.S. Department of the Interior.

COMMUNITY AND ENVIRONMENT

The preservation of this block of historic houses would be a dramatic contribution to the community around the intersection of Columbia Place and Joralemon Street in Brooklyn. It would become an enhanced visual amenity, after the exterior restoration is completed. As a finished product, it would contribute even more. The larger units would meet a burgeoning demand to house modern-day workers needed to fill office buildings in Brooklyn and Manhattan, just as White's tenement dwellers were needed for the smokier industries of his day.

In the proposed design, the interior garden court would be preserved, all dwelling units having views of it and all occupants having access to it. The ground-floor duplexes would enjoy private gardens and the upper-story triplexes would have private rooftop terraces. These upper units would be enhanced by views of the nearby Manhattan skyline and New York Harbor to the west. Existing larger trees on the site would be preserved and the ivy-covered wall facing the highway retained.

ORGANIZATION

In renovating a landmark, the existing volume and skin present an absolute organizing datum. Obviously structure and existing vertical circulation cores are crucial, but it is the form and veneer of historic structures which are given the greatest

Figure 3 *Streetside facade details. A rich combination of materials, openings, and ornament, this elevation evidences the level of craft and art which makes this existing building so worthy of a major revitalization.*

protection and demand the most care. So it is with this immutable given that Kliment and Halsbad have undertaken to completely reinvent a building.

In the broadest sense, this building forms an L shape, and in coincidence with a major highway along its back side, this shape defines a rare urban occurrence—a major backyard. The building also mediates a one-story-level change from street to generous backyard. Internally the original building did not effectively recognize this site feature. Probably due to a desire to simply wedge units within the volume, bathrooms and kitchens plugged much of the visual access to the view. At least the vertical circulation (in the form of attractively curved common stairs) stayed to the street-side, keyed more to ease of access than preservation of the view. The stair-ways also project vertically to form tower elements to the street side of the building facade. Beyond views and circulation, the existing classic bearing-wall building techniques are simply too integral to be obviated.

Thus, Kliment and Halsbad were force-fed an eight-story fixed form internally regulated with bearing walls and stairs whose skin perforations could not significantly change.

Rather than give up easily, and move the nonbearing walls about to effect a spatial response to the need for bigger units, the architects reinvented the building's interior, while leaving the exterior unchanged. Every building has a top, a middle, and a bottom. When these parts are used expressively, buildings manifest their latent potential. When the constituent parts of buildings are ignored, the buildings become underachievers, as evidenced by the internal layout of the existing building on this site.

The architects defined an internal hierarchy where ground-level spaces had the most access and connection to the "backyard" and top spaces had the best view and potential for spatial manipulation, given the available roofscape. Left between earth and air are the middle three floors of this building. The architects used the building's step-down as a means to create a street-accessed duplex for the bottom two floors. The top three floors were treated as the space for a layer of triplex units. The added space afforded by this organization permitted the extraordinary opening up of the middle level of each triplex, creating a double-height living area. These top and bottom layers of multilevel units are to have new interior stairs connecting their interior floors.

"Betwixt and between" these high-amenity units, the middle levels are reconfigured to reduce the total unit quantity by one-third while upping each unit's size by 30 percent. The net result also makes each unit's exterior exposure to the backyard increase by 50 percent.

This scheme is ingenious in that it allows for the revised scheme to follow the structural system of bearing walls, utilizing them for sound sensation as well as unit division, whereas the existing building had a central unit straddling every other bearing wall. These newly recombined middle units provide relatively economical accommodations in the least desirable portion of the building volume.

But the most ingenious aspect of the reworking of the building's interior involves common circulation. The typical rule of thumb is that a four-floor walkup is the maximum tolerable without an elevator. With the ground-level duplex stepping *down* from street level and the top-three floors all one unit, there remain only four runs of stairs to reach the penthouse triplex units—an acceptable cost for the views that the elevation affords. Elevators are thus eliminated, and great cost savings are effected.

It should be noted that no secondary common means of egress can be found in the plans, and this may need negotiations prior to construction.

By relocating all serving components of the projects (bath, kitchen, stairs, closets, utilities) to the middle of the plan for each unit, the appreciation of views is facilitated. The utility of a bearing wall as utility chase organizer is also used.

Figure 4 *Section. This views key understanding of site conditions and building interior utilization. Two opposing vertical elements—building (right) and highway (left)—create a private world of defined exterior space. The eight stories of existing building are cleverly subdivided to create a wide variety of unit types. A garden-level duplex has direct access to the garden. The next three layers are redundant one-level units, the top-three levels create a layer of triplex penthouse units.*

Figure 5 *Courtyard. An elevated walk mediates between the built world (left) and the natural (right). First-story surface and fenestrational variations heighten the sense of the building's responsiveness to those who walk along its edge.*

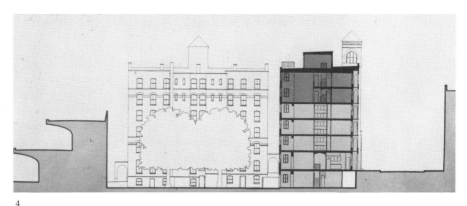

4

5

INTERIORS, AMENITIES, AND SERVICES

A drawing project cannot convey many explicit amenities, but the design approach indicated has many significant positive implications.

Obviously the backyard is a rare commodity in an urban context, and the focus of all units on its presence is a benefit to the occupants. By making an explicit connection with the duplex units, it becomes a major unit enhancement. Similarly, the available views, double-height living spaces, and top-floor terraces combine to make the triplex penthouses worth the aforementioned stair climbing.

This is to be a complete renovation, and involves all new bath and kitchen elements. Typical of New York apartments, these are to be tight in size.

Beyond any new work done or site features present, it is the exquisite skin of the existing building which is a unique and abiding amenity, idiosyncratic enough to have extraordinary value to those who are seduced by its beautiful detailing and proud massing. And so it is with older buildings: The elements which hold the architect at bay are often those which beckon the potential buyer.

EFFICIENCY

Beyond the simple efficiency of common walls and minimized mass, it is not possible to evaluate this criterion without more information.

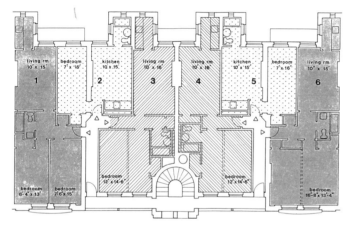

6

Figure 6 *Existing unit plans. The typical unit layout within the existing building was a simple, repeated layering of residential units set above ground-level commercial spaces. Five units belly up to the street-side, single-loaded outdoor corridor springing from a central stair core, which also accommodates utility access. One-and-a-half units exist per bay, with the half unit straddling the bearing-wall system. Wet functions orient to the stair core or are accommodated by the projecting facade bays, effectively limiting appreciation of the courtyard to one window per common space.*

Figure 7 *Proposed Unit Plans. All unit plans respect the given bearing-wall system. The lowest two floors are duplexes. The courtyard level (a1) has a combination living room and master bedroom, and is accessed from the street floor above (a2), which harbors a combination kitchen, dining room, and second bedroom. The middle-three levels (b) are repeated studio apartments with street-facing bedrooms and courtyard-facing public spaces. All wet functions are positioned along the bearing walls. The top-three floors are triplex units, with the lowest level (c2) housing the master bedroom and a sleeping loft overlooking the courtyard side of the public floor. The top level (c3) is a narrow space, recessed from each building edge, which could be used for a bedroom or loft space.*

Photographs Courtesy of the Architects

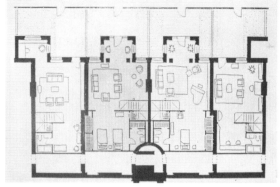

7a1

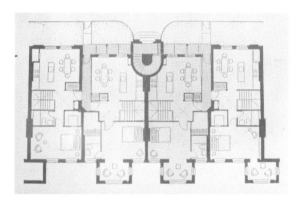

7a2

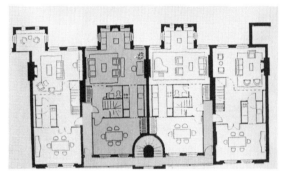

7c1

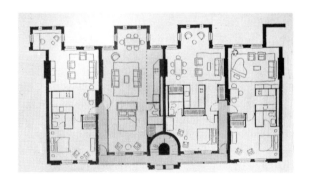

7b

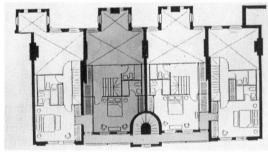

7c2

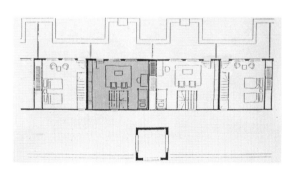

7c3

Density Enhanced by a Clever Residential Pattern

MOTLEY SCHOOL SITE HOUSING

Minneapolis, Minnesota

Mulfinger and Susanka Architects

OBJECTIVES

The architects used their design to enter a competition that was held to determine how this neighborhood school site was to be developed after the old elementary building was demolished. What distinguishes the Mulfinger and Susanka design is the excellent techniques it uses to manage a density of twenty-three units to the acre. Ironically, the design finished second in the competition to a lower-density solution. Despite its relegation to the architect's shelf, the approach teaches us much about how to accomplish affordability through medium-density design in low-rise residential neighborhoods.

The architects studied the adjacent streetscape and found gable-faced detached houses at densities of about 8 to 10 per acre. The streets are punctuated with an occasional small apartment structure. This housing serves a predominantly transient student population of a nearby college and a few homesteading landlords. Into this environment, the architects proposed inserting housing to be sold to faculty members who were single individuals or childless couples, and other similar households.

Along the perimeter of the 2¼-acre site, the architects arranged thirty semidetached homes. Along the side streets approaching the southern corners of the site, these homes are arranged in pairs to resemble larger versions of the other houses on the same streets. Their essential form is nearly identical to the traditional single-family homes nearby, enhanced by upper-story dormers on the sides and lower-story decks and porches. These familiar shapes define the street presentation of the proposed project. Toward the corners, the density is modestly increased by further attaching five of these semidetached buildings and clustering them at a

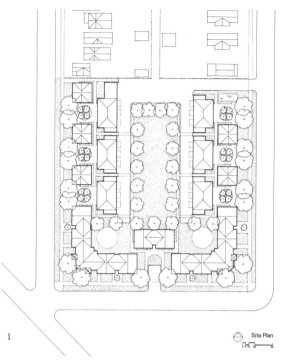

1

Figure 1 *Site. Layers of units interweave with common courtyards, both framing a great public court. The pattern of blocks is used to define a variety of axes, thresholds, and spaces. Crucial to the success of this scheme is the use of Woonerf layer of paved space at the outer ring of the public court, a path designed to accommodate both the strolling pedestrian and the family car.*

Figure 2 *Perspective. Two rows of units mimic the existing fabric of construction in scale, form, and rhythm and create a rare private amenity: the inner common courtyard. Note the left-side view and superimposing edge which follows the street. Note also the dormitory seen in the foreground of this image.*

Site Plan

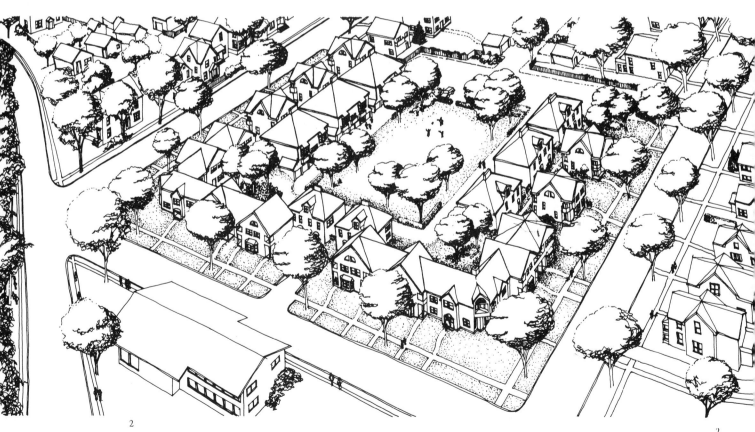

2   2

point where views over a bluff and scenic river are present. The greater density at this end of the block is not at odds with the neighborhood across the street.

Density at a level that enables affordability is accomplished by proposing the construction of an inner ring of residential buildings, each containing two or three individually owned units. The facades and entryways are oriented to the street, giving the passerby a partial view of buildings recessed into the interior of the site offering a continuum of low-scale residential architecture along all three sides of the site. This inner ring of homes is designed around a pastoral inner court, which is an interpretive continuum of the backyards and the alleyways of the homes on the rest of the block.

COMMUNITY AND ENVIRONMENT

The inspiration of this design is its successful effort to triple surrounding densities and yet replicate the community's image. Several ways in which this is done were discussed above. The designers also used other methods to buffer the density and further conform the project to the community and to enhance the environment.

The density of the site is mitigated by the construction below-grade of fifty-seven parking spaces, which reduces the on-grade parking to forty-seven spaces, not greatly in excess of the parking that would be on-grade if the site were built at the density of the rest of the neighborhood. Further, all forty-seven of these above-ground spaces are provided well off the street, largely out of view of the passerby. The entrance to the underground parking is precisely aligned with the alley of the adjacent portion of the block. This is another example of the architects' use of familiar features to accommodate the greater density they envisioned.

Fully three-dozen large trees are arranged around the interior court and the site's perimeter. Significantly, the perimeter trees are placed precisely in front of the facades of the interior residential buildings, so that from the street, a green natural eminence buffers the structural one. This has the effect of echoing the street continuum that is presented along the side streets to the north. Because of this buffering, the visual effect of the recessed homes is not too different from the effect of garages and other accessory structures.

ORGANIZATION

This project presents two clear and well-developed notions of organization applicable to all housing projects. First, formal determination is keyed to the existing scale and rhythms of its neighborhood. Secondly, parking (on a scale completely alien to the project's neighborhood) is treated in ways that make it relatively invisible.

The first design generator, formal integration, was achieved despite the un-precedented density (twenty-three units per acre) imposed on the site. This masking of mass was done by creating a double layer of housing at the site's street edges. It should be noted that the peninsular site—three sides face streets—facilitated many of the moves described in this section.

Perceived mass is often assaulted in projects such as this by a jiggled stepping of form, creating a building no less large but distortingly active and random. The architects for this project had the common sense to break up the mass of their units by true distinctions of form: fourteen freestanding buildings, seven facing the street and seven set in a parallel layer behind the first. Density is further enhanced by making two larger buildings in scale with existing dormitories across the street, addressing the south street side of the site. This simple site-planning notion has the following benefits.

1. *It Echoes the Existing Community Site Geometry.*   By imposing the existing orthogonal grid of street and house orientation, there is both formal and processional continuity with the surrounding condition.

2. *It Creates a Rhythm.*   When these blocks of units are spaced in a manner compatible (dimensionally and in terms of unit mass) with the existing houses, the pattern of units is in harmony with its context.

3. *It Creates Spaces.*   The gaps between units (which so often are unconsidered "leftovers") are given identities in two ways: *(a)* They become courtyards by the centering of the secondary off-street units on their space, and *(b)* they become thresholds by the careful coincidence of the two layers of units' corners.

This simple ordering creates a flow of different scale spaces, with several identities. Eleven of the unit blocks create a "do-si-do" pattern of building-space-building—a checkerboard of mass and space. The other three form an ensemble of two large corner blocks (each equivalent to five do-si-do blocks) set at the two street corners, and a central block set between the corner units on the secondary layer of orientation. This pattern creates three spaces. Between the corner blocks and the second layer are two private backyard spaces. Between the corner blocks and the central block a parking access point and "front door" into the project is created.

Behind the second layer of units is a large courtyard surrounded by trees, a civilized loop for cars and pedestrians, and finally rhythmically spaced blocks. In all, ten distinct spaces are created by fourteen blocks of housing. All blocks are linked and accessible to one another.

Mulfinger & Susanka Architects have embraced the *Woonerf* notion of shared pedestrian and car access space and have applied it to the rear courtyard. The *Woonerf* is a Dutch concept which recognizes where there is no through traffic, and this allows occupant and car coexistence with safety. This functional hierarchy creates a sense of owner (versus car) control of the precious available land.

Despite the density applied to this project, the simple orchestration of space and built form creates buildings with unencumbered views, defined entries, and a significant amount of land given over to occupant use. A common combination of dormers and hipped roof unifies the impression and blends with the surrounding buildings.

The second broad gesture of organization was in the design of the parking for the project. Ninety-five spaces (plus nine for visitors) are virtually invisible from the street and from within the units. Cost and the desire for a natural landscape precluded the raising up of the entire project above a parking garage. But the three southerly units mentioned were set above such a parking accommodation involving fifty-seven spaces, while the remaining east and west do-si-do blocks have their parking set at the level of the great pastoral court, accessed from the Woonerf. These last thirty-eight spaces are set below the inner layer of units and are easily accessible to the outer layer of units facing the street. Visitor parking is accommodated by a simple widening of the Woonerf at the back side of the major courtyard.

It should be noted that virtually all the unit parking is covered and nearly all is directly accessed from the unit interiors.

Weaving space, built form, and parking to create a whole cloth of positive form, defined space, and civilized procession is a difficult task. Why then does this project appear to be an effortless resolution of all those competing desires? A cynic might conclude that its unbuilt status belies its true meaning as a project. In truth, it is the ingenuity of a design team committed to contextual integration and the creation of a community within a community.

INTERIORS, AMENITIES, AND SERVICES

It's hard to get beyond the most general of perceptions in understanding a competition entry's approach to this section heading, but distinct advantages and features have been presented.

All unit entries address the street, with the secondary layer of units accessed via heavily planted courtyards. Plantings are used both to enhance the sense of domesticity and to help define spatial and threshold identities implicit in the various spaces' locations.

The courtyards which are created greatly help to define a series of secure space, all observable and all oriented for active use. The pastoral courtyard and Woonerf employ a scale of space and definition few projects of this size and budget can match.

Double-height spaces, duplex and triplex units with lofts, and raised living areas create a sense of spatial variety. Bedrooms, kitchen, and baths are all small, as are the closets, but there are dens, recreation rooms, and in most units, laundries. Some units have decks, others bay windows.

Trash removal and grounds maintenance were part of the proposal's presented strategy.

EFFICIENCY

Minnesota is cold in the winter. The use of "super insulation" (deep walls), high-efficiency triple-pane glazing, and airlocks were intended to minimize heat loss.

Several types of insulation were to be employed, and the basic units' massing into cubic volumes is inherently energy-conserving.

West Elevation

3

Figure 4 *Parking. Underground spaces at bottom, Woonerf-accessed spaces flank the great court, while visitor spaces stand exposed at the top of the courtyard.*

Figure 5 *Unit layout. Dark-gray rectangles indicate each duplex or triplex row-house unit.*

Figure 6 *Unit Plans. A variety of unit plans respect a bearing-wall structural system. The units have a variety of configurations—duplexes, triplexes, and four-level schemes, if basements are included. Stairs are located along bearing walls either at corners, unit centers, or as straight-run laminations. Four corner units use a diagonal wall to create a specialized response to a unique site condition.*

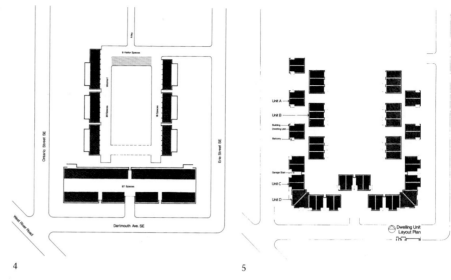

4

5

6a

6b

6c

6d

Figure 3 *Elevation. Three sets of blocks face the street, with a secondary layer of recessed block sets in the center. To the right, attached units form corners addressing the streetscape. To the left the existing freestanding single-family homes key the scale, detailing, and rhythms of the new construction.*

A Glimpse of the Year 2000

VEST POCKET COMMUNITY
Fairfax, California
Daniel Solomon & Associates, *Architects*

OBJECTIVES

The operative question for this proposed development is whether it is ahead of its time, and yet dead-on-target for the special housing needs of the next generation. A simple description of what the architects and their nonprofit developer-sponsor want to accomplish suffices to explain how different it is.

On less than an acre, the architects have designed six moderately large houses, configured to accommodate, together, a total of twenty-four households. This involves an average of four households living in each separate house. The number of households per acre is thirty, and yet the number of houses per acre is seven. Bathrooms are shared by two households; living rooms, kitchens, and dining rooms by four; and community rooms by twelve.

How is a zoning or planning board to react to such a scheme? How would the market react?

What Daniel Solomon, the architect, and Innovative Housing, the sponsor, have proposed is a microcosm of what is known generically as "congregate housing." In such housing, usually on a much larger scale, elderly or handicapped individuals are provided small individual apartments and encouraged to socialize in amenable common spaces, such as congregate dining rooms, community rooms, or recreational areas. Life-care facilities for the elderly, nursing homes, special hospitals for the handicapped, and other highly specialized residential and supportive communities have been built in this way for quite some time.

More recently a smaller-scale version of congregate housing has developed. With the deinstitutionalization of marginally mentally ill and developmentally disabled persons in some states, there has been a desire to integrate such individuals into traditional living situations, namely, the single-family neighborhood. Although such small developments are routinely and vigorously opposed by their

Figure 1 *Site. A two-lot site, joined by the incidence of two streets. The lower cluster of three units center on the common parking area and gathering place, and sit upon a relatively level site. The upper-four units are splayed about a common axis that runs uphill to a common court and axially located barbecue. Parking for these units is located under the lower-two units. Note that the central crossaxial courtyards of both unit clusters serve as primary entry areas.*

Figure 2 *Upper cluster. Four units are axially arrayed, and crossaxially accessed as they march up the hill. Common roof detailing, large-scale openings, massing articulations, and material palette unify this cluster's identity and link it with its lower cousin across the street.*

1

2

neighbors, on average they tend to be successful habitats for their occupants and eventually win acceptance in the community.

A similar, less controversial, mode of small-scale congregate housing has emerged in a few communities. Here, a few independent elderly individuals each purchase one unit in a quadriplex home which, from the street, looks like a large single-family home, but in reality is four separate units. Because of the fewer cars owned by the elderly, and the generally lighter use they make of their residences, these multifamily prototypes tend to look like, and have the neighborhood impact of, a single-family home.

In yet another context, "tandem homes" have been offered to the market to allow unrelated single individuals to pool their resources to purchase a typical single-family home, on the outside, that operates quite uniquely inside. Tandem homes, typically, have two large master bedrooms, at remote ends of the structure, to ensure privacy, with perhaps a small adjoining den or sitting room. Single living, dining, kitchen, and utility spaces are provided to be shared by each of the bread-winning occupant-owners.

The Solomon proposal moves these small-scale models one step closer to their large-scale counterparts. In Vest Pocket Community, the individual rooms are kept small and offer the only truly private space to the occupants. Communitywide interchange is clearly emphasized in the design, through the community room, a shared outdoor courtyard, a common garden, a mutual dining arbor and barbecue, and a shared parking area. Within each house, shared living is the norm, with one floor devoted to individual sleeping rooms, and the other to common living space.

To our knowledge, this specific congregate housing concept is untested in the planning boardroom and the residential marketplace. And, yet, the demographic studies cited throughout this book foretell a tremendous demand for this or some similar concept. The shortage of capital for new development, the limitations of natural resources for building, the limitations on earning power for vast segments of our population, combined with the trend toward one- and two-person families, all recommend such models for serious future consideration.

COMMUNITY AND ENVIRONMENT

In addition to overcoming doubt about its innovativeness, this project must hurdle all the routine barriers that confront traditional developments.

The biggest physical impact of any development on the site, in this particular neighborhood, is traffic, which is of great concern to the neighbors. How many cars will these twenty-four households have? When will the occupants leave and return, and how often? How does one study the traffic impact of similar projects when there are none?

In Fairfax, it was determined that this living arrangement of four to six unrelated individuals, sharing a kitchen and living area, is "family" under the zoning ordinance, qualifying the structures as single-family houses, thereby legal in the district. In the legal sense, then, this innovative concept has conformed to the norms of the community.

The sponsor proposes removing an auto repair garage and small church from the site, and building a development using a single-family motif. This physical use of the site is not unusual, and does fit the character of the environs.

Like any serious effort of this sort, Vest Pocket Community was subjected to evaluation by neighborhood residents. The architects and sponsor have made adjustments in the design and reduced the density, at least twice, in response to community design and traffic concerns. As we go to press, this process continues so that we might learn whether this project, too, is a prologue to the future or an idea whose time has come.

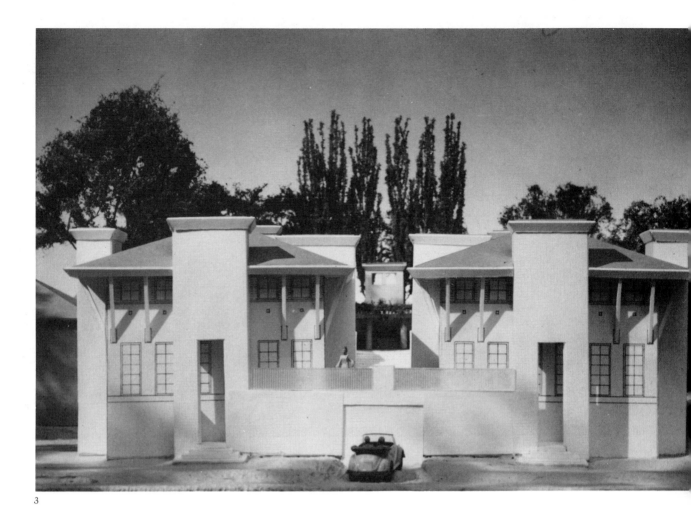

3

Figure 3 *Upper cluster axis. Mirror facades center on a common parking axis. The vertical projections define a great formal threshold. The distant prospect of a celebrated barbecue flue provides a cross-site axial linkage. The broad eaves, vertical massing counterpoints, window organization, and ornamental trim serve to create a depth of scale rarely seen in a residential project of this size. Common pedestrian access from the street is accommodated by common stairs set in the flanking tower elements.*

Figure 4 *Upper cluster elevation. This hillside view shows the site slope which had to be accommodated, and the common detailing which engenders a unified ambience. The lower units address the major street and sit above parking, upper units sit between the street and the common barbecue court. Between the units, a common pedestrian threshold is created, and some parking is accommodated under the upper unit. This elevation addresses the minor street which terminates across from the common parking/public space.*

4

5

Figure 5 *Lower cluster. Three units address a common parking lot, which doubles as the spatial fulcrum for the entire project. Note how the vertical plan projections form thresholds and focal points while harboring unit entries.*

Figure 6 *Lower cluster elevations. Three distinct units create an ensemble of parts, defining thresholds and creating spaces. Vertical elements create focal points and are counterpoints to horizontal eave lines. Note the use of materials and scale of detailing.*

6

ORGANIZATION

Buildings can be organized in a variety of ways, addressing need, site, and art with varying degrees of priority. There are few projects in this book which present a better mingling of these design criteria. The programmatic focus of this project has a marvelous impact on the buildings' plan and form. Two kitty-corner lots—one sloping, one flat—allow for a decompressed site plan. The seven separate buildings quietly subdivide their individual lots while creating a cross-referential connection between the two plots of land. Lastly, the applied motifs and detailing create an aesthetic image which is both invigorated and yet decidedly residential.

This project benefits from an extraordinary perspective; its programmatic forces are thoroughly innovative. But Daniel Solomon and Associates allowed this conceptual innovation to fertilize their design sensibility as well. Confronted with the desire to create extended-family accommodation, the architects simply refused to knuckle under to the easy solutions. They might have provided dormitory-style accommodations, or perhaps traditional flats with more bedrooms and larger social areas. Instead, these plans are reinvented by their design program. Each building contains one social area with common living, dining, study, and kitchen spaces. Bedrooms, by necessity more secluded than in normal construction, stake out corners, or are nestled between bathrooms. Stairs and entries are effected on a grander scale, approaching a small public building in size. Some bedrooms have sinks, but share common toilet and tubs, still others have their own bath, which is also commonly accessible. Public spaces of different functions run into one another, facilitating the possibility for very large social gatherings. Kitchens are spread out, making possible multiple meal preparations. In short, intimacy and a larger social sense mingle, creating a midpoint between public and private accommodation.

All planning principles are effected in seven buildings, designed in three types but all utilizing a 6 by 6 foot planning grid overlay—a quiet, but insistently consistent ordering device. Symmetry is also used by two of the three block types.

All these design criteria occur in concert with a binary site—two lots diagonally linked by proximate corners. The parking adapts to each and organizes the buildings set upon each site piece. The lower, flat site has a triadic array of buildings: one long, a "wall" building, and two with an L configuration. The L's are mirrored to create a threshold to the parking area, which dominates close to half the lot's area. This threshold becomes the middle of a major site axis, terminating the long building's central axis. A secondary cross axis parallels the long, or wall, building. These clear site-planning gestures create an inner court between the three buildings and yet afford open access to the surrounding community.

The site's impact on this scheme is best measured by the upper, sloping lot whose long-side lot line aligns with the short-side lot line of the lower site. This alignment is enhanced by consistent use of trees whose rhythmic planting spans the street separating the lots, forming an implicit threshold. This upper lot has four units set in an axially symmetric array. The lower units (L's, as in the triad of the lower lot) also form a threshold. These two units sit atop a subterranean parking lot, accessed from the street which separates the two lots. Two upper buildings—which are a third type, made up of simple rectangles mirrored to each other—have their short and outside long walls parallel to lower L blocks. Since each parallel block duet parallels the skewed side lot lines, an ever-widening axis is created. The upper units have a continuous parking area span under their lower end which may be accessed from the side street.

Culminating this ascending opening lot is a minipark, complete with barbecue. The happy happenstance of a curving upper end to the lot helps to reinforce the special identity of this focal space. The cross axis between upper- and lower-unit types is celebrated with a minor courtyard that harbors access stairs to the subterranean parking garages.

It is in the orientation of the lower lot's parking area that these two subtextual communities are linked. This scheme recognizes the now-traditional function of parking lots as public gathering places.

The two sites, thus wedded, spawn buildings of differing context and orientation. But these buildings have identical roof pitch, use of materials, and large-scale ornamental detailing of hugely extended eaves and roof brackets. Window type and organization is also consistent. An extraordinary effort is made to create vertical counterpoints to the dominant horizontal massing of the units by utilizing chimneylike vertical projections which accommodate stairs, sleeping porches, and entries. Large-scale patterning and banding of surface materials and windows also enliven the building facades and serve to refresh the simple building forms.

It is the consistent manipulation of a wide-ranging palette of details, materials, and shapes which allow an atypical site to be unified. Large-scale site developments form a context that gives order to disparate lot characteristics and allows seven separate buildings to act in concert. The breadth and depth of vision so cogently applied to the possibilities present in this scheme can be used in any project of this scale, no matter what particular needs are addressed.

INTERIORS, AMENITIES, AND SERVICES

As mentioned earlier, the particular programmatic needs of congregate living create some specialized amenities. Large-scale public spaces and kitchens, alternative bath organizations, and idiosyncratic spaces such as sleeping porches and open studies help manifest the possibilities of shared-living accommodation.

This project allows for open planning to occur without the loss of personal scale. This is done in two ways. First, the largest public areas are *lightly* subdivided by freestanding wall pieces rather than by heavily defining doorways. Secondly, the bedrooms are personalized by private elements—vanities, sleeping porches, built-in desks.

In the symmetrical "wall" and "rectangle" buildings, large focal fireplaces mated with staircases addressing common rooms are a centering influence. The L unit has an inglenook fireplace and a stair bypassed by the point of entry. (The stair is made special by the only curve present in the entire project.) The complementary interior layouts present distinct approaches to public and private space planning. The L units have one central bath for the four bedrooms; the wall and rectangular units have two baths, plus separate vanities for all four bedrooms. The L and rectangular buildings have separate first-floor bedrooms with semiprivate baths. The wall building has the most open, grand public space, the L has the most easily bypassed public space, and the rectangle has the most segmented living spaces.

All bedrooms have angled or cathedral ceilings and are nestled under the extraordinary eaves.

Though unbuilt, this project has designed durability and flexibility into the bath and kitchen spaces. Finishes, however, are as yet undetermined.

EFFICIENCY

There is no cogent information in this area, save that in San Francisco's mild climate, temperature is not a dominant design problem, and the aggrandized eave conditions should effectively obviate the muddy season's local impact.

Figure 7 *Unit plans. The "wall" unit (a) of the lower triad cluster a uses a central entry, stair, and fireplace to order both floors. The upper floor has four bedrooms and two common baths. Each bedroom has its own sink. The corner unit (b) occurs in both upper and lower sites and forms the major axis threshold for each. Public functions are held distinct from the minor on-grade bedroom intended for the handicapped. All four second-floor bedrooms are different. Note the one curve that is used in the entire project—the beckoning stair landing. The "rectangular" unit (c) has an on-grade handicapped bedroom and four identical bedrooms. Bilateral symmetry organizes the unit's spaces and circulation.*

Photographs Courtesy of the Architects

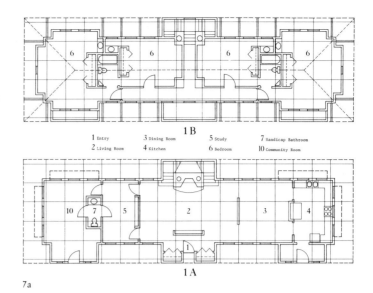

1 Entry 3 Dining Room 5 Study 7 Handicap Bathroom
2 Living Room 4 Kitchen 6 Bedroom 10 Community Room

7a

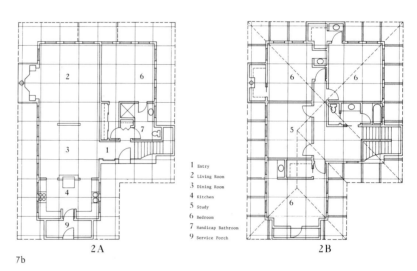

1 Entry
2 Living Room
3 Dining Room
4 Kitchen
5 Study
6 Bedroom
7 Handicap Bathroom
9 Service Porch

7b

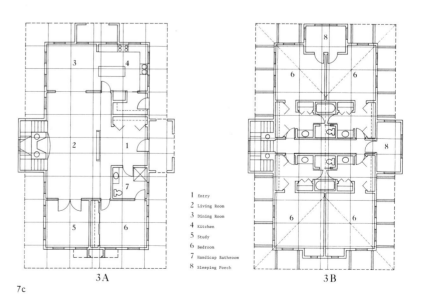

1 Entry
2 Living Room
3 Dining Room
4 Kitchen
5 Study
6 Bedroom
7 Handicap Bathroom
8 Sleeping Porch

7c

Design Conclusions

If this book gives evidence of a hopeful future for the art and science of attached-housing design, it is important to summarize the essential lessons that can be drawn from the examples studied. In these pages, the authors found certain recurring principles common to all the designs which qualified for publication. By following these principles, the architects invariably enhanced their projects; often these same principles gave the project its aesthetic backbone and essential appeal.

1. *Create Exterior Space.* Attached housing can create well-defined and visually exciting spaces when the architecture employed meshes with the site. The fact is that the scale of the architecture employed must have a datum, or minimum amount, of exterior space to be successful. The creation of meaningful space requires attention to the sequences of circulation, focal points, and hierarchy of spatial definition.

2. *Celebrate Circulation.* Gaining access to a site and processing through it and into the living unit presents the greatest challenge to humanizing attached housing. By its very nature, attached housing is a less personal and more abstract method of human accommodation than its single-family counterpart. By careful manipulation of circulation to create entry thresholds, internal vistas, and well-defined focal points and subspaces, the architect can make the pedestrian and occupant feel

comfortable. It is not inherently expensive to order circulation in a way that entices those who encounter the project.

Project thresholds and unit thresholds need to be articulated in such a way that they are inviting and yet have enough integrity of image to be residential in character. Level changes, axial orientations, the adaption to natural phenomenon, and the inspired use of detail and material can all be employed to enhance the act of circulation.

3. *Respect the Natural or Contextual Surroundings.*   Whether set in an urban fabric or on a site with mature trees, a large-scale building of any type can become a misfit unless careful attention is paid to maintaining the natural habitat and to respecting the existing patterns, rhythms, and social imagery of the surrounding community. Architecture must be rooted in context or it will lose its ability to touch those who must live under its influence.

4. *Create Thresholds, Axes, and Focal Points.*   Whether in terms of formal massing, circulation, space, or the respect for a given system of contextual aesthetics or natural phenomenon, the need to provide for human movement is crucial. The act of access is given added meaning by the creation of a threshold. When a threshold is continued by the act of circulation or visual connection in the form of axes, a sequence is given depth and large-scale meaning. When those two elements are received by a focal point (either of space, mass, or object), the sequence is concluded. This creation of beginning, middle, and end is applicable to the largest considerations of site design, down through the level of unit planning, and even down to the personal scale of individual room design.

5. *Explicitly Apply an Ordering System or Systems.*   The norm in attached housing is a random stepping and meandering massing which is intended to give units individuality, but more often creates an arbitrary and inconsistent sense of design. The ragged chaos of movement for movement's sake is simply gratuitous. Such stepping and movement has disastrous consequences in terms of durability and cost.

The projects in this book evidence clear and integrated hierarchically ordered systems. Predominantly rectilinear, buildings are also organized by existing natural and constructed contexts. By mimicking the rational sense or architectural order found in most "traditional" communities, the expressive or interpretive gestures made by the architect are given a positive sense of perspective. This principle can be applied to all other principles previously discussed.

6. *Pay Attention to Material, Detail, Color, and Surface.*   Although attached housing is inherently large-scale relative to single-family detached housing, its use by individuals is the same as that of a freestanding home. A human scale and fit is a design imperative for successful housing of all kinds.

Although it has been assumed to be expensive to use natural materials or enriching ornament, some of the most visually rich projects in this book have the lowest cost per square foot. This is due to the design priorities of the architect which accommodates such vitalizing detail in the spatial and functional imperative imposed upon the project. Small-scale visual and sensory amenities create a sense of pride and ownership in their occupants. The positive implications in terms of maintenance, utility, and longevity are obvious.

7. *Recognize Specialized Use Groups.* Rather than apply any given pallet of materials and details to any given group of users, the best attached-housing projects determine features in concert with the nature of those who will be using them. This can mean a recognition of the past in housing for the elderly, a celebration of the family in low-income housing, or simply the integration of the two-income lifestyle of the average housing consumer. When image is keyed to use, the domestic ambience reaches its highest potential.

8. *Integrate Form and Facade.* Designing large-scale massing and fenestration articulations to act in concert to reinforce the basic project image has obvious benefits from both distant and internal vantages. Attached-housing projects of the scale and programmatic versatility evidenced in this book can create expressive and invigorated massing, complemented and enhanced by stimulating window and door patterning. When acting in concert with the material and detail potentials addressed earlier, the results can be quite powerful.

All the projects in this book are places where people live. They are houses harboring several, dozens, or hundreds of people. Houses are not civic buildings, or laboratories for aesthetic or social engineering. Houses are the most essential and most personal of human possessions. If a building does not convey the scale, detail, and spatial ambience of domestic life, its occupants will seldom feel embraced by its presence. When attached housing fails to convey the common ground of a shared living environment, then no matter what aesthetic, technical, or social innovations are attempted, the project must be viewed as a fundamental failure. All the projects in this book artfully convey the fact that they are, in truth, houses.

This book attempts to show the housing consumer, the housing designer, and the housing producer that economy and innovation can walk hand in hand without sacrificing utility. If these principles are adhered to, attached-housing projects can become the new villages of the coming generation. These villages can recognize the individual occupants and the common large-scale ordering features which make their image both cogent and inspiring. The diversity of housing type, location, and approach is intended to underline the applicability of these design criteria. The questionnaire described in the following section assists in the further exploration of these principles. They help us learn how to achieve density without preempting the dignity of habitation present in all these projects.

Introduction to the Design Criteria

To evaluate each of the projects submitted for possible inclusion in this book, the authors used an extensive list of design criteria, which is cited in full in this chapter. The list is organized in the same way as each of the preceding sections. The design criteria begin with a look at each project's objectives, then at its community compatibility, and then at its environmental fit. After that, the organization of the site plan, the interiors, and finally the efficiency of the projects are scrutinized. Under each of these six categories, there is a long list of features and options to be considered.

Part catalog and part procedural chart, this list of criteria references the reader to the broad spectrum of design elements which have an impact on the creation of residential developments. Architects might find in it a sense of the potential paths addressed by a given project's aesthetics. Builders might find a sense of perspective between marketing concerns and the other key aspects of a project's character. Housing consumers might gain an overview of the multitude of factors which help form each of the case studies featured in this book.

This list of design criteria was used as an aid in drafting the questionnaire that was sent to the architects of each of the featured projects and was helpful in developing the design conclusions contained in the preceding section.

DESIGN CRITERIA

A. Objectives

1. Demographics
   a. Analysis
   b. Targeting
   c. Marketing
2. Financing
   a. Pro forma analysis
   b. Technique(s)
      (1) Private
      (2) Bank
      (3) Institution
      (4) Government
         (a) Loan
         (b) Grant
      (5) Sequencing
         (a) Interim
         (b) Construction, zoning leverage points
         (c) Refinancing
3. Dwelling type and capacity (see D)
4. Costs
   a. Tenure or ownership type
      (1) Own lot
      (2) Own unit only
      (3) Own side yards
      (4) Rental
      (5) Cooperative
      (6) Joint tenancy
      (7) Tenancy in common
      (8) Partnership
      (9) Limited partnership
      (10) Corporate
      (11) Home Owner's Association
   b. Cost-reduction features
      (1) Prefab units
      (2) Modular units
      (3) Component construction
      (4) Snap togethers
      (5) Framing kit
      (6) Plastic pipe
      (7) Wood foundations
      (8) Standardized plans
      (9) Design for minimum built space or mass
      (10) Siting to reduce cost
         (a) Zero lot line
         (b) Shared amenity or infrastructure
      (11) Materials used
      (12) Specifications or tolerances set to reduce cost
      (13) Technological ingenuity
      (14) Computer-aided design
5. Marketing
   a. Appropriateness of unit type
   b. Project image
   c. Owner or other innovative financing
   d. Warranties
   e. Unit amenities (see E)
   f. Site amenities (see C)
   g. Services offered (see D)

B. Community

1. Accessibility: Analysis of existing conditions
   a. Infrastructure
   b. Traffic
   c. Transportation systems
   d. Job centers
   e. Worship centers

f. Shopping centers

g. Schools

h. Parking requirements

  (1) Resident

  (2) Visitor, services

i. Movement patterns

  (1) Pedestrian

    (a) Handicapped

    (b) Elderly

    (c) Children

  (2) Vehicular

    (a) Resident

    (b) Visitor

    (c) Emergency

    (d) Service

2. Congruity

  a. Integration with existing community

    (1) Social implications, image

    (2) Political: Local and state regulations

      (a) Building code

      (b) Fire code

      (c) Zoning regulations

      (d) Historic districts

      (e) Wetlands

      (f) Enterprise zones

  b. Aesthetic impact on existing community

    (1) Rehabilitation/reuse of existing on-site structures

    (2) Massing

      (a) Rhythm

      (b) Scale

      (c) Geometry

      (d) Detailing

      (e) Style

      (f) Materials

    (3) Integration with existing site use

    (4) Use of site amenities for community use

      (a) Pedestrian accommodation

      (b) Parking

      (c) Park, nature preserve

      (d) Playground

      (e) Commercial and business elements

      (f) Lighting

      (g) Recreational or sports facility

      (h) Rehabilitation of existing buildings

C. Environment

1. Minimization of disturbance

  a. Coastline

  b. Trees

  c. Topography

  d. Views

  e. Impervious coverage

  f. Foundation type

  g. Nature of paths, streets

  h. Ground-water loss or retention

  i. Stream or river path

2. Use of special phenomena

  a. Views

  b. Water

  c. Terrain

  d. Weather

    (1) Snow

    (2) Sunlight

  e. Urban fabric

3. Relationship to existing conditions

  a. Use of indigenous materials

  b. Use of indigenous foliage

  c. Use of on-site water

  d. Use of wind

  e. Use of sun

f. Views

g. Reuse, rehabilitations of existing structures

4. Implications of existing natural phenomena

   a. Subsoil conditions

     (1) Bearing capacity: structural

     (2) Water table: infrastructure/utility

   b. Temperature variations

     (1) Wall section detail (see F)

     (2) Expansion or contraction detailing

     (3) Material selection

     (4) Mass/fenestration orientation

   c. Rainfall and snowfall

     (1) Roof type

     (2) Runoff accommodation

   d. Grade

     (1) Vehicular or pedestrian access and parking

     (2) Structural/massing compatibility with slope

   e. Earthquake

     (1) Structural detailing

     (2) Geometric accommodation

   f. High wind

     (1) Glazing

       (a) Size

       (b) Location

       (c) Type

     (2) Structural detailing

     (3) Geometric orientation

D. Organization

1. Generative patterns

   a. Interaction with on-site rehabbed buildings

   b. Contextual: Massing

     (1) Heights

     (2) Setbacks

     (3) Geometries

       (a) Roofscapes

       (b) Walls

       (c) Rhythmic elements

   c. Contextual: Imagery

     (1) Historic

     (2) Allusive

     (3) Innovative

   d. Structural

     (1) Spans

     (2) Supports

     (3) Grids

     (4) Bearing lines

   e. Programmatic: Densities

     (1) People

     (2) Cars

   f. Programmatic: Functional accommodation

     (1) Service

     (2) Commercial

     (3) Recreational

   g. Aesthetic

     (1) Massing forms

       (a) Symmetrical

       (b) Organic

       (c) Historic, allusive, innovative

     (2) Patterns

       (a) Geometric

         • Orthogonal

         • Polygonal

         • Radial

       (b) Organic

       (c) Allusive

       (d) Eclectic, multigenerative

     (3) Rhythms

       (a) Natural (trees and foliage)

       (b) Built (material, detailing, structure)

     (4) material implications

(a) Structural systems

(b) Environmental and weathering

(c) Historic, allusive, metaphoric

h. Circulation

(1) Pedestrian

(2) Vehicular

i. Spatial

(1) Functional

(a) Points of access, gateways

(b) Entries

(c) Play, gathering, sport

(d) Public or common space

(e) Private yard

(2) Response to view

(3) Parking

j. Perception

(1) Distant prospect

(2) Gateway

(3) Subgrouping and cluster identification

2. Building type

a. Slab

b. Low-rise

c. Mid-rise

d. High-rise

e. Tower

f. Needle tower

g. Courtyard

h. Cluster

i. Town house

j. Garden apartment

k. Bermed or buried

l. Megastructural

m. Terrace

n. Wall building

o. Urban block

p. Urban in-fill

3. Systematic

a. Circulation

(1) Pedestrian

(2) Vehicular

(a) Resident

(b) Visitor

(c) Community nonresident or nonvisitor

(d) Emergency

(e) Service

b. Security

(1) Complex

(2) Unit

c. Infrastructure

(1) Street system

(2) Utility access

(3) Right-of-way accommodation

(4) Transportation system access

4. Site conditions (see C)

5. Energy conservation (see F)

E. Interiors, Amenities, and Services

1. Unit size

a. Actual square footage

b. Perceived square footage

(1) Double-height space

(2) Axial spatial orientation

(3) Size and orientation of openings

(4) Inside/outside orientations

2. Circulation-to-occupiable space ratio

3. Storage-to-occupiable space ratio

4. Parking

a. Quantity

(1) Resident

(2) Visitor

b. Type

(1) Heated, enclosed

(2) Unheated, enclosed

(3) Attached carport

(4) Detached carport

(5) Parking lot

c. Proximity

5. Accentuated features

  a. Kitchen

    (1) Size

    (2) Appliances

    (3) Finishes

  b. Master bedroom

    (1) Size

    (2) Bath

      (a) Size

      (b) Fixtures

      (c) Finishes

    (3) Closet

      (a) Size

      (b) Organizational systems

  c. Living space

    (1) Size

    (2) Outside access

    (3) Fireplaces

    (4) Surfaces

  d. Specific features

    (1) Communication equipment

    (2) Appliances

    (3) Lighting

    (4) Technological amenities

    (5) Materials

    (6) Security

    (7) Accommodation of handicapped and elderly

    (8) Low maintenance

    (9) Energy efficiency (see F)

    (10) Services offered

      (a) Day care

      (b) Concierge

      (c) Security

      (d) Lawn, garden

      (e) Trash removal and site cleanliness

(f) Laundry

6. Site feature

  a. Built ancillary amenity

    (1) Sports/health

    (2) Day care, schools

    (3) Meeting

    (4) Service

    (5) Security

  b. Natural (see C)

F. Efficiency

1. Orientation

  a. Massing, shape

    (1) Wind collection or avoidance

    (2) Shading

    (3) Minimizing radiational surface area

  b. Solar access

  c. Openings

    (1) Wind

    (2) Cooling

    (3) Solar gain

    (4) Daylighting

2. Technological assistance

  a. Insulation, thermal breaks

  b. Controls

  c. Heat plant efficiency

3. Design

  a. Airlocks

  b. Massing reduction

  c. Use of eaves

    (1) Shading

    (2) Wind collection or avoidance

    (3) Minimizing runoff effects

  d. Window: skylighting for daylighting

  e. Reduction of volume of interior spaces

  f. Plan organization for appropriate light and heat levels

The Questionnaire

Derived from our list of design criteria, this questionnaire served as a datum by which contributing architects could communicate the nonvisual aspects of their projects to the authors for the purposes of preliminary evaluation, and the subsequent writing of each article. Approximately forty projects were selected to receive questionnaires, out of over 200 project submissions. The final twenty-two selections were made based on the information presented by the responses to these questions, as well as the quality and quantity of graphic material submitted.

The authors found that while most architects were happy to fill out the questionnaire, some were not well-versed on all the aspects covered. We took care of this problem by conducting direct follow-up interviews. As the architects thought and wrote about their projects, they offered very few additions to the listings of features or to the questions posed. Most of them were impressed with the completeness of the perspective this questionnaire offered. The questionnaire served, too, as a useful method for them to cross-reference the other written and graphic material they submitted.

When read in conjunction with the design criteria, this questionnaire offers a fairly broad and inclusive overview of any attached-housing project. The builder, architect, developer, and housing consumer might all benefit from a quick run-through of this questionnaire, as it attempts to address a multitude of site and social conditions, as well as the aesthetic and procedural features common to all attached-housing projects.

PRELIMINARY QUESTIONNAIRE
FOR POTENTIAL PROJECTS

This questionnaire is designed to do two things: convey information for review by the authors and integrate all projects in a common evaluative matrix.

The series of questions we will ask shall progress through the following overview of project sequence:

A. BASIC STATISTICS
- the essential facts of your project

B. OBJECTIVES
- What is the conceptual basis of your project?
- Whom does it serve?
- How does it meet the needs of those it serves?

C. COMMUNITY
- Where is this project, geographically, socially?
- What infrastructural elements existed or needed to be built?

D. ENVIRONMENT
- What natural elements were utilized or overcome by your project?
- What were the methods used and costs imposed in the adaptation of your project to the natural environs?

E. ORGANIZATION
- How many ways is your project organized, and what is the hierarchical importance of these organizing systems?
- Are these organizing systems/features of your project evident in the nature of construction or aesthetics employed?

F. INTERIORS, AMENITIES, AND SERVICES
- What features of your project are employed for the enhancement of the living environment?
- What impact do these features have on cost and organization?

G. EFFICIENCY
- In terms of energy use, how well does the project conserve power or fuel?
- How do the organizational or environmental aspects of the project impact on efficiency?

A. BASIC STATISTICS

1. Name of Project _____

2. Location _____

3. Name of developing company/organization _____

4. Architect _____

5. Builder _____

6. Total project cost _____ . Date completed _____

7. Percent of total space built new _____ . Percent rehabbed _____

8. Give your best guess at a budget breakdown:
   - Percent of cost spent on land acquisition _____
   - Percent of cost spent on site development _____
   - Percent of cost spent on infrastructure _____
   - Percent of cost spent on construction of units _____
   - Percent of cost spent on construction of amenity buildings _____
   - Percent of cost spent on marketing _____
   - Percent of cost spent on debt service _____

9. Cost per square foot, heated, finished space, including all costs listed above, except land acquisition _____

10. Total acreage of site _____

11. Density (units per acre) _____

12. Unit quantities: Studio _____ One BR _____ Two BR _____ Three BR _____ More than three BR. Define and list quantities _____

13. Prices: Studio $ _____ One BR $ _____ Two BR $ _____ Three BR $ _____ More than three BR, define and price _____

14. Maintenance/dues per unit: Studio _____ One BR _____ Two BR _____ Three BR _____ More than three BR, define and give cost _____

15. Square footages: Studio _____ One BR _____ Two BR _____ Three BR _____ More than three BR. Define and size _____

16. Number of parking spaces per unit _____

B. OBJECTIVES

17. What income group (or groups) was this project intended to attract/serve?

18. What demographic group (or groups) was this project intended to attract/serve (double income/no kids, empty nesters, single professionals)? Rank your groups in order of priority.

19. Was there an analysis of targeted group behavior patterns, and if so, how were the results of such analysis integrated with the building design and subsequent cost analysis? _____ If yes, explain: _____

20. How were prices of the units derived? _____

21. What cost-cutting measures were used, if any, to meet this market? _____

22. What political/social circumstances affected project planning? _____

23. Was there a master plan of image/marketing derived from the factors listed above, or were the factors above derived from a preset master plan? In either case, review the generative or resultant master plan/concept/image: _____

24. Did the developer provide any warranty to the purchasers? If so, describe the terms:

25. Were units (check one) _____ rented, _____ sold. If sold, were the units sold as _____ a cooperative, _____ a condominium, _____ part of homeowner association.

26. What property management features were used to market the project? _____

27. Describe the nature of the financing used to underwrite the project. Address the sequencing of project development as it affected the type of financing used. ___

C. COMMUNITY

28. Size of town/city/village of location (population) _____

29. Describe the image/character of the surrounding community _____

30. What role did the existing aesthetics of the surrounding community or existing buildings on site play in the derivation of the project's design? _____

31. What governmental restrictions (zoning, fire, building code) impacted on the final project concept, form, and approach? Describe the extent of impact these restrictions had on the project. _____

32. What community response greeted the original development proposal? _____

33. What response was made in the demographic, marketing, and design focus to the community reaction to the original project proposal? _____

34. Major pedestrian or vehicular access points/methods used in project _____

35. Type of parking: relationship to access and existing community _____

36. Relationship of public spaces to parking and existing community _____

D. ENVIRONMENT

37. Natural and environmental features encountered _____

38. Natural and environmental features modified or removed _____

39. Natural and environmental features preserved and enhanced _____

40. Materials utilized which related to indigenous environment _____

41. Massing and orientation of project in response to natural or environmental conditions _____

42. Check off those areas which had impact on the final design:

_____ Solar gain

_____ Runoff

_____ Shading

_____ Slope

_____ View

_____ Winds

_____ Water (lake, river)

_____ Earthquake

Others _____

Describe the impact of those areas checked off _____

E. ORGANIZATION

43. Did existing patterns of building massing/aesthetics in the community determine the final building form or organization? If so, how? _____

44. How did vehicular access and parking help determine the design generation of the scheme? _____

45. How did the exterior form of the project serve to organize the entire design of the project? _____

46. How do exterior views organize the project? _____

47. How do public spaces organize the project? _____

48. How does pedestrian access organize the project? _____

49. Did existing on-site buildings help organize the project? If so, how? _____

50. Check off those areas which had impact on the final design organization:

_____ Security

_____ Gateways

_____ Distant prospect

_____ Applied geometry

_____ Structural systems

_____ Low maintenance

_____ Interior spatial organization

_____ Private exterior spaces

_____ Infrastructural questions

_____ Ancillary amenities (clubhouses, tennis courts, etc.)

_____ Energy efficiency

_____ Density/lot coverage

_____ Others

How did these areas checked off affect the organization of the project? _____

F. INTERIORS, AMENITIES, AND SERVICES

51. Describe storage (excluding garage space) as a percentage of total project area

52. Does the project have (check one) _____ heated _____ unheated garage; or carport _____ parking space _____

53. Check off those features which had an impact on the design:

_____ Kitchens

_____ Baths

_____ Heating/cooling systems

_____ High-tech appliances/fixtures (describe)

_____ Fireplaces

_____ Soundproofing

_____ Daylighting

_____ Double-height spaces

_____ Axial spaces/organization

_____ Decks, balconies

_____ Openings (doors, windows, etc.)

_____ Level changes

_____ Exterior views as seen from interior spaces

_____ Low maintenance

_____ Surface treatments

_____ Closet/storage organization

Others _____

Describe how these features affected the design of the project _____

54. Are there any on-site ancillary buildings or site developments which are used to enhance the appeal of the project? How do they respond to the targeted demographic occupancy group and basic project image/objective? _____

55. Check off the amenities offered in this project:

_____ Day care

_____ Concierge

_____ Lawn and garden maintenance

_____ Unit interior maintenance

_____ Shuttle bus service

_____ On-site nurse

_____ On-site security force

_____ Trash removal

Other _____

How did the accommodation of these services affect the design of the project?

G. EFFICIENCY

56. How does the project design (from site to unit) minimize energy cost? _____

57. Does the natural terrain enhance energy efficiency? _____

58. What types of insulation are used in the project? _____

59. Check those areas of the project used to enhance energy efficiency:

_____ Design to avoid air filtration (describe)

_____ Design to avoid heat radiation (describe)

_____ Use of wind

_____ Shading

_____ Passive solar gain

_____ Active solar gain

_____ Water (as storage/flywheel, or power generator)

_____ High-tech elements (heat plants, hot water heaters, energy controls, glazing type, lighting elements, computer regulation/monitoring)

_____ Daylighting

Other _____

How were these features employed in the design of the project and the development and implementation of a marketing plan? _____

Addendum

Are there any considerations, constraints, or objectives which have not been addressed in this questionnaire? If so, please use this page to identify and describe those omissions, and talk about how these features or factors had an impact on the development and implementation of the project.

Index

ABOUT THE AUTHORS

John Nolon is a professor of real estate law at Pace Law School in New York, specializing in land planning, housing and regional development. He has consulted on many innovative residential development projects and has participated in the President's Council on Development Choices for the 1980s.

Duo Dickinson is a registered architect in Connecticut with his own practice in residential and light commercial design. Winner of one of *Architectural Record's* prestigious Period House Awards design in 1985, he is also the author of two critically acclaimed books, *Adding On* and *The Small House*, both published by McGraw-Hill. He is currently a visiting critic in design at Yale and is on the adjunct faculty of Roger Williams College.